Elite • 171

American Civil War Railroad Tactics

ROBERT R. HODGES JR. ILLUSTRATED BY PETER DENNIS

Consultant editor Martin Windrow

First published in Great Britain in 2009 by Osprey Publishing,
Midland House, West Way, Botley, Oxford OX2 0PH, UK
443 Park Avenue South, New York, NY 10016, USA
Email: **info@ospreypublishing.com**

Print ISBN: 978 1 84603 452 7
ebook ISBN: 978 1 84603 889 1

Editor: Martin Windrow
Design: Ken Vail Graphic Design, Cambridge, UK (kvgd.com)
Typeset in Sabon and Myriad Pro
Index by Fineline Editorial Services
Originated by PPS Grasmere, Leeds, UK
Printed in China through World Print Ltd.

09 10 9 8 7 6 5 4 3 2 1

A CIP catalog record for this book is available from the British Library

PHOTOGRAPHIC CREDITS

The illustrations referenced "LC" are courtesy of the Library of Congress.

ARTIST'S NOTE

Readers may care to note that the original paintings from which the colour plates in this book were prepared are available for private sale. All reproduction copyright whatsoever is retained by the Publishers. All enquiries should be addressed to:

Peter Dennis, Fieldhead, The Park, Mansfield, Notts NG18 2AT, UK

The Publishers regret that they can enter into no correspondence upon this matter.

CONTENTS

INTRODUCTION 4
The American railroad system in 1861

HARNESSING THE IRON HORSE FOR WAR 7
The Union: the Railways and Telegraph Act – McCallum and Haupt
The Confederacy: the Railroad Bureau - state resistance to centralization

MOVING THE INFANTRY 12
Johnston at First Manassas – Jackson in the Shenandoah Valley – Bragg at Chattanooga and Chickamauga – McClellan on the Peninsula – Burnside in North Carolina

RAIL BATTERIES 17
Heavy batteries: Lee's "Dry Land *Merrimac*" – Magruder at Galveston – Finegan in Florida – Light batteries: howitzer cars – ironclads

WRECKING THE RAILROADS 29

REPAIRING THE RAILROADS 32

RUNNING THE RAILROADS 38
Workforces: the black contribution – water – fuel – wear and tear – the telegraph – fortifications

TRAINS IN BATTLE 44
Troops versus trains: ambush – deliberate engagement
Reconnaissance – balloons – command cars – handcars

HOSPITAL TRAINS 54
Evacuation – mobile hospitals

FURTHER READING 62

INDEX 64

AMERICAN CIVIL WAR RAILROAD TACTICS

INTRODUCTION

The American Civil War is widely regarded as the world's first major railroad war. Railroads moved troops over hundreds of miles, and served as vital lifelines to armies in the field. Major battles were fought for control of crucial Southern rail centers such as Chattanooga, Atlanta, Richmond and neighboring Petersburg. Although the vast logistical role played by railroads has received much attention from historians, their tactical capacity has been comparatively overlooked. At the outbreak of hostilities the steam-powered locomotive was the world's fastest land vehicle; it was widely available, and military commanders quickly exploited this resource to its fullest capacity. Rail vehicles provided rapid troop insertion and extraction; they

A Hayes 4-6-0 "camelback" locomotive built in 1853. At 30 tons, these hefty engines could pull heavy coal and freight loads through mountainous regions. They also provided plenty of power for the Union "ironclad" trains, although the high cab put the engine crews in greater danger from Confederate small-arms and artillery fire. (Courtesy Baltimore & Ohio Railroad Museum)

US Military Railroads nine-stake flatcars at City Point, VA, where the USMRR built an impressive logistics center for the operations around Petersburg. While engine crews loved to have their locomotives photographed, the humble freight cars often went neglected. At the time these flats were termed "platform" cars, and it was a simple task to turn a freight-hauler into a rolling weapon-platform. (LC)

were employed for command, reconnaissance, and medical evacuation; they assisted in "commando-style" raids, and they maintained lines of communication when no other option was available. On many occasions trains functioned as rolling (and sometimes armored) weapons platforms. In terms of tactical versatility in their period, it is no exaggeration to compare Civil War rail vehicles with American helicopters in Vietnam.

The nature of the railroad system

By 1861 some 30,000 miles of railroad lines crossed the American landscape, of which about 9,000 miles were in what would soon become the Confederacy. Although the South actually had more track mileage per capita, the relatively industrialized North's amount of equipment, rolling stock, and factory capacity to produce new trains far outstripped those of carriers in the rural South.

The era of American railroads had begun in the late 1820s and really boomed in the 1850s. They were built for the most part by private investors for commercial purposes; over 100 railroad companies existed in the South alone, and companies across the country were fiercely competitive. A few state governments either owned or effectively controlled their own lines, and both city and county governments managed to funnel money into rail projects by offering tax rebates or guaranteeing bonds in order to entice railroad companies to build in their area, in the hope of increasing local commerce and tax revenues. State and local governments were just as competitive as the private companies, and a major result of all this competition was a lack of connecting lines. Many owners did not want to see their rolling stock heading

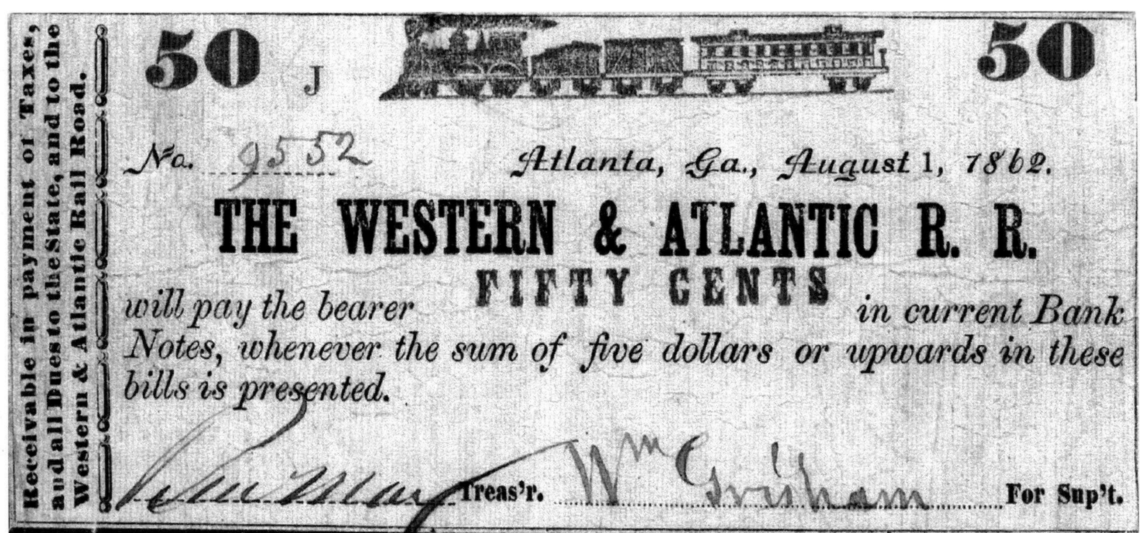

A 50-cent note issued by the state-owned and -operated Western & Atlantic Railroad based in Atlanta, GA. Many banks and large capital-holding companies such as the railroads, as well as a few cities and counties, issued their own currency notes. On both these and the currency issued by individual Southern states trains were a common motif, since they symbolized commerce and prosperity. The W & A, one of the principal lines utilized by Sherman during his march through Georgia, had earlier been the scene of the famous "Great Locomotive Chase," when disguised Northerners led by Capt James Andrews hijacked the locomotive *The General* and a train of cars. Conductor W.A. Fuller used more than one locomotive, a pole car and his own feet to chase the Federals, and finally recovered *The General*. The fully restored locomotive now rests in the Southern Museum in Kennesaw, GA. (Author's collection)

down a competitor's line, perhaps never to return. Richmond, for example, had five rail lines entering the city, but none of them were physically connected, thus condemning passengers and freight to time-wasting transfers before they could resume their journeys.

Another consequence was the complete absence of standardization. In both North and South, track gauges ranged from 4ft 8½in to 6ft, thus preventing the transfer of rolling stock from one line to the next. Many companies built their railroads as cheaply as possible, with flimsy rails and poorly ballasted roadbeds. Most trains traveled along iron "T-rails," but a number of tracks still consisted of the old-style strap iron – a thin strip of iron, fixed to a wooden stringer with U-shaped strips. Safety standards on American railroads were often well below those on their European counterparts; in 1860 alone nearly 600 Americans died in railroad accidents, the majority of them company employees.

The typical locomotive of the day was the American type 4-4-0, although some companies – such as the Baltimore & Ohio, which pulled heavy coal loads out of mountainous regions – also invested in more powerful eight-wheel and ten-wheel engines. The steam-driven engine commonly used cordwood for fuel, although by this date some companies had already switched to coal. The crucial eight-wheel sheet-iron tender, coupled just behind the engine, carried the fuel and water, and when loaded often weighed as much as the engine itself. Depending on the speed and other conditions, a locomotive could travel about 25 miles on one cord of wood and 1,000 gallons of water – the average load for tenders of the day, although some were built with twice that capacity.

Wartime rolling stock included boxcars, flatcars, open-topped cattle cars, hoppers, gondolas, and dump cars. Except for some coal cars and a few iron boxcars most had wooden bodies, including passenger cars. Sometimes these had a longer life than their iron counterparts, which were highly susceptible to rust – the tender, essentially a rolling iron water tank, rarely lasted more than ten years in use. Wooden passenger cars did have one major drawback, however: a serious accident would shatter them in a murderous storm of flying glass and jagged splinters.

HARNESSING THE IRON HORSE FOR WAR

When war erupted, both sides scrambled to turn the disjointed private rail networks into viable military transportation systems. Both governments were aided by the fact that many of their senior commanders had been railroad men before the war (graduates of West Point, especially to the Corps of Engineers, were highly sought-after), but were impeded by the fact that many corrupt politicians owned railroad companies. To a large extent the railroad companies retained their autonomy and kept their civilian employees while assisting the military; however, in January 1862 the US Congress passed the Railways and Telegraph Act, giving President Lincoln sweeping powers over all railroads in the United States. Under this Act the government could requisition for military use any line and any piece of railroad or telegraph equipment in the country, and could impress any railroad or telegraph employee for service in a war zone.

The following month Lincoln appointed Daniel C. McCallum as military director of railroads, in charge of the newly created United States Military Railroads. While financially dependent on the Quartermaster General, McCallum, a former supervisor on the New York & Erie Railroad, had control of the daily operations of his department. During the course of the war the USMRR would buy, build or capture 419 locomotives and 6,330 cars in addition to the rolling stock already requisitioned from Northern railroads. The USMRR built their own line connecting Washington DC with Alexandria, Virginia, as well as a line extending from City Point to the siege

Brigadier General Herman Haupt, the technical brains behind the USMRR, photographed while making a typically hands-on personal inspection, here by means of a raft with inflated rubber floats. Among his many other innovations Haupt put together a series of photographs and written instructions demonstrating how to twist rails, blow bridges, and repair them; he circulated copies among Union commanders, who sometimes took the credit for the results achieved by using Haupt's ideas. (LC)

operations at Petersburg, Virginia. Altogether McCallum's department would eventually control more than 2,000 miles of mostly Southern track.

The real technical brains of the department were provided by Herman Haupt, serving under McCallum as chief of the Construction Corps. Haupt had graduated from West Point in 1835, but almost immediately resigned his commission to pursue a successful career in railroading. He became a skilled and innovative civil engineer and architect, and he literally wrote the book on bridge construction. In April 1862, at the request of US Secretary of War Edwin Stanton, Haupt returned to the US Army in the rank of colonel and was later promoted to brigadier-general. Haupt's hands-on approach greatly improved USMRR operations, and he was quick to pass on his knowledge and expertise to his fellow officers.

South of the Mason-Dixon Line, Confederate railroaders were just as active. The Confederate government established a special department within the Quartermaster Bureau to deal with railroad concerns and to liaise between the central government, the private carriers and the various state governments. Eventually known as the Railroad Bureau, it went through several chiefs during its existence, including William A. Ashe, William M. Wadley, and Frederick W. Sims. All three men had held senior positions with railroad companies, and each would have made great improvements to the efficiency of the Southern rail network if he had only been granted the power to do so, but all were hampered by Southern political attitudes. Southern states typically mistrusted a powerful central government and wanted to keep decision-making closer to home. President Jefferson Davis' administration tried several times to pass a bill comparable to that which had given Lincoln total military control over the Northern railroads, but the Confederate Congress absolutely rejected this until it was far too late to have any benefit – such a bill was finally passed in late February 1865, only weeks before Robert E. Lee would surrender at Appomattox.

During the war some lines were recognized as strategically vital while others, through damage or merely due to location, were effectively useless.

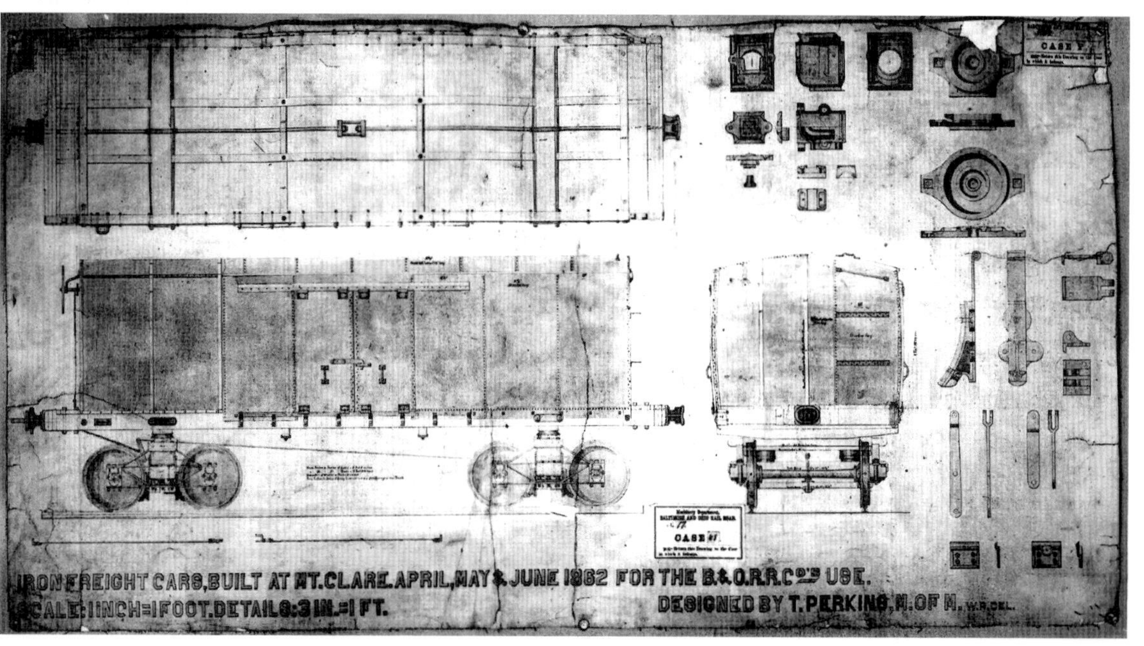

A wartime plan of a fairly rare iron boxcar design. While most carriers were using wooden boxcars before and during the war the B & O experimented with an iron model, and their shops built 104 of these during the course of the war. They were originally used to haul barrels of flour, but as the demands of the US Army increased they were pressed into general freight service. (Courtesy B & O Railroad Museum)

This photograph of a Civil War-era B & O iron boxcar was taken in 1927; the company restored several cars while preparing for their centennial celebration. The sliding doors are missing, giving a good view of the inner doors. Note the brakeman's hand wheel and ladder. Several boxcars and coal cars of Civil War vintage can still be seen today at the B & O Railroad Museum in Baltimore, MD. (Courtesy B & O Railroad Museum)

On one occasion Ashe, under direct orders from Secretary of War Judah P. Benjamin, set out to borrow or seize six locomotives and 70 boxcars from the state-owned Western & Atlantic Railroad of Georgia in order to move freight out of eastern Tennessee. Georgia Governor Joseph E. Brown was so incensed that he threatened to send Georgia troops to fight any Confederate officials interfering with his cars or engines; Secretary Benjamin had to rescind his order, and valuable government freight remained bottled up in Tennessee.

On another occasion, the Confederate government wanted to construct a line connecting Florida with Georgia; Florida was a major beef supplier for the Confederate Army and the government needed a swifter means of moving loads out of the state. The Railroad Bureau suffered from a shortage of rail iron; the Federal blockade made it difficult to obtain from Britain, and the Confederate Navy took 1,100 tons of rails for use on their ironclad ships. Old lines had to be cannibalized to build new tracks; the Florida Railroad had already suffered damage, and with inadequate rolling stock it was less important than the new connecting line. Despite this pressing military need David L. Yulee, president of the Florida Railroad, refused to cooperate (although the army took his rails anyway).

Despite the lack of labor and materials, and the difficulties with state and local officials and private companies, the Confederate government managed to build numerous connecting lines along some critical state borders and even within city centers. The South also managed to repair damaged rolling stock, kept essential lines running, and captured quantities of equipment and materials (including rails) from the North. Many of the military innovations on Confederate railroads came at the insistence of Gen Robert E. Lee.

A USMRR locomotive and tender at a watering station at City Point. Even in this wartime scene the luster of the metalwork on the jacket and even the domes is clearly visible; someone has taken the time to polish this army workhorse. A 4-4-0 locomotive cost about $10,000 – an important sum. The two men in the foreground are sitting on an upturned pole car. Note the fairly haphazard spacing of the crossties (sleepers) of the track in the foreground. (LC)

A

LOCOMOTIVES

1: AMERICAN TYPE 4-4-0 "GENERAL MCCALLUM"

By the 1850s-60s locomotives were highly decorated, and the engines and tenders built specifically for the military were no exception; the staid gray and black colorschemes often seen after the Civil War would have been a novelty in the 1860s. From the fireman earning a dollar a day to the company president, railroad men were proud of their machines, and celebrated their pride by decorating engines with paintings of pastoral scenes, Greek gods and goddesses, city architecture and, of course, portraits – of railroad men, generals and wartime politicians. Like ships, captured engines were usually renamed to reflect their new owner's patriotism. Bright paint and varnish adorned the locomotives, set off by arrays of polished brass and copper. While boiler jackets often went unpainted, workers would polish the iron to a shine. Some felt that the metal finery was a waste of money, but brass did last longer than iron (which soon rusted, despite protective paint), and a shiny engine was easier to see in dark, rainy conditions, which made it safer. Economics would eventually win out over aesthetics; for example, the Philadelphia & Reading spent $285 a day paying employees to polish more than 400 engines, so by the end of the century brightly polished engines were a thing of the past. The American type 4-4-0 engine and tender seen here was named after Brevet BrigGen Daniel C. McCallum, military director of the US Military Railroads.

2: ARMORED LOCOMOTIVE "TALISMAN"

This experimental armored Union engine utilizes 3/8in iron plate to protect the cab and some of the working parts. The armor was designed to resist bullets but not artillery fire; according to an 1863 article in the *Scientific American*, "they would stay the progress of a shell no better than so much brown paper." Small arms fire was unlikely to pierce both the iron jacket and the wood insulation between the jacket and the boiler itself, but could puncture the water tank in the tender, and here a shell has punched through the thin metal of the smokestack. Some period photographs show locomotives completely wrecked by artillery fire.

3: HOSPITAL TRAIN LOCOMOTIVE, UNION ARMY OF THE CUMBERLAND

The Army of the Cumberland enjoyed excellent railroad equipment and service; this engine pulled one of the three hospital trains operating in 1864. Major General George Thomas, the army commander, allowed his senior medical director, Dr George Cooper, to choose the best locomotives and cars available to serve as hospital trains. Their smokestacks, cabs and tenders were painted a bright scarlet to prevent Confederates from shooting at them, and at night they ran with three red lanterns suspended from the headlamp. The boiler jacket is shown in a popular finish, unpainted but highly polished "Russian gray." (These are not exactly scaled engineering drawings. All the locomotives illustrated were approximately 41 feet long, plus about 19 feet for the tender, and the smokestacks rose to about 19 feet above the track.)

1

2

3

The busy City Point railroad yard, where Federal matériel could be transferred efficiently between supply vessels on the James River and the troops in the trenches around Petersburg, VA. Trains and horse-teams coming and going on the riverbank, and the transport ships bringing in rolling stock and supplies, are all visible in this view. The boxcars in the foreground appear well worn. (LC)

Although a lifelong soldier and not a railroad man before the war, Lee was quick to recognize the importance of speedy rail transportation; he had already used trains to rush US Marines to Harper's Ferry to put down John Brown's raid in October 1859. Virginia seceded from the Union on April 17, 1861, and Lee accepted command of the Virginia forces six days later. Almost immediately he called for the defense of threatened railroads in northern Virginia, but within weeks Lee judged the Orange & Alexandria and the Manassas Gap lines hopeless; he ordered the evacuation of important equipment and managed to save most of their locomotives and cars.

MOVING THE INFANTRY

Under ideal track conditions a steam locomotive could reach speeds in excess of 60mph, though such conditions hardly ever existed on American railroads. Normal peacetime operating speeds were between 15 and 25mph, and under wartime conditions – with track and rolling stock receiving poor maintenance, and with an ever-present threat of enemy sabotage – trains in the embattled South ran as slowly as 6mph on some lines. Even so, trains could still deliver in a matter of hours the troops and supplies that would normally take days to arrive by wagon and on foot. Troops disembarking from a train were also more rested and battle-ready than their comrades coming off a long road march. In spite of the worsening track conditions, dilapidated equipment, varying gauges, and unconnected lines, field commanders still pulled off some spectacular troop movements.

First Manassas and the Valley Campaign

A famous example of rail movement altering the course of a battle came early, at First Manassas on July 21, 1861. General P.G.T. Beauregard's outnumbered Confederates were falling back until elements of Joseph E. Johnston's army helped to check and then rout the Union forces. Johnston, stationed in the Shenandoah Valley, loaded his men onto cars of the Manassas Gap Railroad and sent them east over the Blue Ridge Mountains to support Beauregard. Early on July 18 "Stonewall" Jackson's brigade led the way to the station at Piedmont for the 34-mile rail journey to Manassas Junction, followed by those of BrigGens Bartow and Bee. When Jackson reached Piedmont at 6am on July 19 only one train was available, but another was commandeered on the 20th. All three brigades had been shuttled east by the time the battle opened early on the 21st, and the arrival late that afternoon of E. Kirby Smith's 2,000 men was finally decisive.

Nearly a year later, "Stonewall" Jackson used both fast marching and trains to confuse and then defeat three separate Union armies during his Shenandoah Valley Campaign. In early May 1862 he marched his "foot cavalry" out of the Valley to Mechum's River Station on the Virginia Central line, loaded his men onto the cars and sent them straight back into the Valley, to the surprise of everyone including his own officers.

Moving the infantry: MajGen Christopher Augur's Federal troops waiting to catch a ride back to their camp at Upton's Hill, VA. These heavily laden troops are not burdened with military equipment but rather with loot from local homes. The reclining soldiers beyond the drummer-boy, left background, seem to be resting on a railroad pole car. (LC)

The Peninsula and North Carolina

If trains brought troops to battle, sometimes the troops brought the trains. While MajGen George B. McClellan was busy landing his 105,000-man army on the Virginia Peninsula in March 1862, he ordered the USMRR to load five locomotives and 80 cars aboard ships and have them placed on standby in Baltimore harbor. McClellan (formerly chief engineer of the Illinois Central Railroad, and president of the Ohio & Mississippi) planned to use the existing lines in Virginia for his advance on Richmond and, anticipating that the Confederates would pull back their trains ahead of him, he knew he would need his own. In late May, with the Peninsular campaign well under way, McClellan landed the first of his engines and cars at White House Landing, where – after making repairs – he could utilize the Richmond & York River Railroad. In June a sixth engine completed his inventory, all these being purchased from Northern companies. When McClellan retreated at the close of his unsuccessful invasion, he left behind all the engines and cars in a damaged condition.

Coordinating with McClellan's threat on Richmond, MajGen Ambrose Burnside (a former colleague of McClellan's with the Illinois Central) launched a landing on the North Carolina mainland at New Berne. On March 14 his ground troops and gunboats pounded New Berne's unfinished defenses; after a stiff fight the North Carolinians fell back to the city, where they boarded cars and retreated by rail to Kinston. Thereafter Burnside's problem proved not to be getting into New Berne, but getting out. Like McClellan, he planned to use the local rail system but, unlike McClellan, he

A variety of vessels were used by the North to transport rolling stock to various military districts along the waterways. Here, two barges are carrying eight loaded USMRR boxcars to Aquia Creek Landing. (LC)

did not enjoy the full cooperation of the War Department. The Atlantic & North Carolina line stretched from Morehead City south of New Berne to Goldsborough, and his superiors urged Burnside to move on Goldsborough. Although he had the troops to stab further inland he lacked the transportation to supply them; storms at Hatteras had killed so many of his horses that he only had enough left for 20 or 25 wagons. For three months he begged the War Department to send him locomotives and cars (though his amphibious troops did bring along some handcars, which proved useful in unloading supplies.) In June 1862 the War Department finally managed to ship Burnside four locomotives and 50 cars from Baltimore, but two of these engines went to the bottom when a schooner sank in a gale at Hatteras Inlet. They were replaced, and Burnside also received another 50 cars.

Chattanooga

Some of the war's largest troop movements by rail centered on the fighting around Chattanooga. Anticipating a Federal attack on eastern Tennessee in June 1862, Gen Braxton Bragg, commanding the Army of the Mississippi, decided to rush his troops to Chattanooga to support E. Kirby Smith's men who were coming down from Knoxville. From there they planned to make thrusts into Kentucky and disrupt Federal communications, but first they had to secure Chattanooga before Union MajGen Don Carlos Buell could forestall them. The only available rail route between Bragg's headquarters in Tupelo, MS, and Chattanooga involved a circuitous ride south to Mobile, then north and east via Atlanta. Bragg, not ready to commit his entire army to the rickety rails, sent one division first as a test; six days later 3,000 Confederates steamed safely into Chattanooga, and Bragg was convinced. In late July he ordered the artillery, supply wagons, engineers, and cavalry to move overland, while his infantrymen were issued seven days' cooked rations and placed aboard the trains. The regiments' departure was staggered to prevent major loss from any single disaster, and in the event they arrived without a snag. In all, Bragg had moved 25,000 men 776 miles by rail, using six different carriers.

Chickamauga and its aftermath

During the campaigning the following summer, Bragg abandoned the "Gateway City" while he danced around Union MajGen William S. Rosecrans' Army of the Cumberland. Bragg called for reinforcements; in early September, Gen Lee felt he could spare James Longstreet for the time being, so the First Corps (minus Pickett's division, so badly mauled at Gettysburg two months earlier) prepared to detach from the Army of Northern Virginia and ride the rails. The first elements of nine infantry brigades and an artillery battalion – at least 12,000 men – left on September 9, 1863; some boarded trains as far away as Orange Court House, while others marched to Richmond or Petersburg to catch a ride. To relieve rail congestion the Railroad Bureau broke up the corps, sending several brigades to the Georgia-Tennessee border via Wilmington; others went through Charlotte, and 1,200 men went as far south as Savannah. Sixteen different railroads participated in the movement, and by September 18–19 around half of Longstreet's infantry had arrived, just in time to help Bragg hammer Rosecrans at the battle of Chickamauga. The artillery, bringing up the rear, puffed into Ringgold Station near Chattanooga on September 25 after an 843-mile trek; some of the infantry units had traveled well over 900

A view of Burnside's Wharf, built while Ambrose Burnside was commanding the Army of the Potomac. Situated a mile and a half from Aquia Creek Landing, the wharf was connected to the Richmond, Fredericksburg & Potomac Railroad, and could offload both trains and wagons. (LC)

harrowing miles on cheap Southern tracks that had never been intended for such heavy work. In the words of Longstreet's aide-de-camp, Gilbert Moxley Sorrel: "Never before were so many troops moved over such worn-out railways, none first-class from the beginning. Never before were such crazy cars – passenger, baggage, mail, coal, box, platform, all and every sort wobbling on the jumping strap-iron – used for hauling good soldiers."

Rosecrans fell back to Chattanooga while the Confederates occupied the surrounding high ground. Using their cavalry, they were able to smash incoming Union supply convoys. With the Tennessee River at his back and Bragg's army to his front Rosecrans was trapped, and his men literally faced starvation. Following the example of their adversaries, the War Department in Washington decided to launch its own grandiose troop movement to save the battered Army of the Cumberland. George Gordon Meade, then commanding the Army of the Potomac, was ordered to give up two corps for detached duty. He selected two of his least prized formations for this relief force – the largely German XI Corps, which had also been badly chewed up at Gettysburg, and XII Corps – and his least popular subordinate to command them: "Fighting Joe" Hooker, who was detested by some of his fellow officers. Popular or not, they would prove their worth. On September 25 the first elements steamed out of Washington, and within 11 days the trains had dropped ten batteries of light artillery, a hundred carloads of war supplies and 20,000 troops within striking distance of Chattanooga. Meanwhile, a second relief force got under way from Vicksburg. On October 3 some 17,000 Federals under the command of William T. Sherman boarded steamers and headed up the Mississippi River to Memphis, where they climbed onto cars on the Memphis & Charleston line. Unlike their comrades in the XI and XII Corps, who rode on slightly better equipment and took a slightly safer route, Sherman's men were riding on a severely war-damaged Southern line which had to be repaired along the way, and it took them six weeks to reach their destination.

RAIL BATTERIES

Railroad "batteries" – the term in this context meaning single pieces of ordnance – were common during the Civil War. Mortars, howitzers, field guns, swivel guns, and huge naval guns were all mounted on railroad cars and sent into battle; some were armored, some shielded, and some had little or no protection. Some were built on contract in the safety of company workshops and delivered to the military like any other piece of rolling stock, while others were constructed more or less in the field. Civil War commanders were truly inventing mechanized warfare as they went along, and consequently their railborne combat vehicles were often ones-of-a-kind, lacking any sort of official military designation. However, one can reasonably divide them into heavy and light categories.

HEAVY BATTERIES

Robert E. Lee's "Dry Land *Merrimac*" is often cited as the world's first railroad battery to see combat. As McClellan advanced up the Virginia

The most significant use of heavy rail batteries by Union forces occurred during essentially siege operations such as the Petersburg campaign of 1864–65. The railroads were an excellent way to move heavy guns into position, and the Union rail batteries could roll out to bombard Confederate earthworks before retiring to safety. This front view of such a weapon shows that the embrasure allowed some leeway for the gun's elevation, if not for traverse. It is unclear from this image whether or not the face of the sloping shield, bolted onto the thick wooden beams and planking, is covered with rolled iron strips. (LC)

Peninsula in 1862, taking control of the Richmond & York River Railroad near the Chickahominy River, he constructed "blinds" along the roadbed to conceal his operations. General Lee surmised that McClellan might even be constructing a railroad battery behind the screening, and therefore decided to confront the possible threat with a weapon of his own. On June 5, Lee asked Chief of Ordnance Josiah Gorgas to coordinate with the CS Navy in constructing an iron-plated car. Lieutenant John M. Brooke – one of the principal designers in the conversion of the fire-gutted hull of the USS *Merrimac* into the ironclad CSS *Virginia* – also designed Lee's land-based ironclad, hence its somewhat facetious name. Since the Navy built the ironclad car, Lee requested that Secretary of the Navy Stephen R. Mallory have naval personnel man it; in fact, although the crew selected were not sailors, they had served with the navy (and, by a remarkable coincidence, even aboard the real *Merrimac*.)

Rear view of the same railroad battery near Petersburg. It probably mounts a 32-pdr; the top of the siege carriage is visible. Like the Confederate "Dry Land *Merrimac*," this battery features seven axles and a thick wooden casemate, but unlike that pioneering weapon its sides are exposed.

B LEE'S "DRY LAND *MERRIMAC*"; SAVAGE'S STATION, VIRGINIA, JUNE 1862

An artist's impression of the Confederate heavy battery that went into action on June 29, 1862 at Savage's Station on the Virginia Peninsula, commanded by Lt James E. Barry. Built by the same yard and to similar specifications as the superstructure of a Confederate ironclad ship, it featured an 18in wooden casemate and an iron skin and apron. The open top and back provided ventilation as well as a quick escape route for the crew. Since Lee expected it to combat heavy Union guns also mounted on railroad cars, it may have had as much armor plating as its naval namesake: a 2in inner layer of 6in-wide rolled iron strips fixed horizontally, and a 2in outer layer secured vertically. When the CS Navy delivered the railroad battery, with its rifled and banded 32-pdr, they also provided 200 rounds of ammunition including 15in solid bolt shot. According to one account, the Land *Merrimac* weighed around 60 tons, making it nearly three times heavier than the locomotive propelling it (while the engine lacked armor, it did have a protective layer of cotton bales fixed to the cab.) After Savage's Station, Union prisoners were shocked by the moving gun and asked their captors how they transported it, to which the Confederates jokingly replied, "by forty horses." The Land *Merrimac* held up well against small arms and field artillery, but the roadbed, locomotive and tender were another matter.

The highly versatile United Artillery of Norfolk, then stationed at Fort Norfolk, were trained as light artillery, heavy artillery, and infantry, and while they fought in all those capacities they also served on board Confederate ships. When the Navy was about to launch the CSS *Virginia* into action they lacked the sailors to man all her guns, so they called for volunteers. The United Artillery flatly refused to serve under naval officers, and the Navy Department didn't care which officers they served under so long as they served. The company then volunteered to a man, but only 31 were selected along with their own officers. Now Lt James E. Barry, Sgt Daniel Knowles, and 13 men would comprise the crew of the land version, while N. S. Walker, a York River Railroad engineer, volunteered to drive them into battle. On June 24, 1862 the battery was officially handed over to the Army; however, on its "maiden voyage" one of the timbers under the heavy 32-pdr gun broke, and it was June 28 before the Confederacy's latest oddity chugged down the tracks again from Richmond, on its way to its historic debut at the battle of Savage's Station.

On June 29 heavy fighting once again broke out on the Peninsula as McClellan pulled his army back toward the James River; Lee pressed forward, ordering MajGen John B. Magruder's division to spearhead the assault along the Nine Mile road. With steam up, Lt Barry sat within the Confederate lines about 6 miles from Richmond awaiting orders, and at around 10am Magruder sent him forward. After a mile the battery had to stop for some time to clear away heavy obstructions left on the tracks by the retreating Federals. When it had pushed forward to a point near the clearing by Savage's house the rail battery stopped for the engineer to speak with BrigGen Richard Griffith; suddenly, a Union shell burst next to the armored car and mortally wounded the Mississippi brigadier. The "Land *Merrimac*" immediately rumbled forward and, with its much larger shells, silenced the

June 29, 1862: the battle of Savage's Station. The explosions and fires show where the Federals are destroying their own ammunition trains. Down the tracks to the left, about halfway between the explosion and the edge, another puff of smoke may be the artist's attempt to indicate the location of Gen Lee's "Dry Land *Merrimac*." At the right are Federal hospital tents. (LC)

Union battery before firing on the woods nearby. Later that afternoon the rail battery was sent forward with Confederate skirmishers, and fired into several Union positions including a train. The Federals were forming a line of battle in Savage's field, and Magruder ordered Barry to move a quarter-mile closer and fire on them. After a couple of rounds the Union infantry scattered into the woods and regrouped. More infantry poured into the woods in support, and a battery of Federal Parrot guns opened up on the "Land *Merrimac.*" With the locomotive completely exposed, Barry had to pull back under an absolute hail of fire, but under their thick armor the gun car crew were completely unscathed. Although this experimental weapon had its share of detractors it did prove rather effective. According to a Union signal officer, "the range and service of the piece were splendid, and its fire was most annoying." A Union prisoner who was captured that day estimated that the iron monster killed or wounded 100 men and 30 horses.

Magruder certainly had faith in the concept, because he had a heavy battery built in Galveston after his transfer to Texas. Magruder hoped to liberate the occupied city by a bold attack using boats, the railroad, artillery and infantry. The Federals were not heavily invested in Galveston, and their main force consisted of six gunboats in the bay including the USS *Harriet Lane,* with a couple of hundred infantrymen on the wharves. At one point they had planned to destroy the 2-mile long railroad bridge connecting Galveston Island with the Texas mainland by ramming it with a burning ship, and they would later regret having changed their minds. Under cover of darkness, Magruder used the railroad to transport six siege guns into the city and distribute them near the wharf; an additional 14 field pieces and the railroad battery would complete his artillery. Lacking the means to construct iron plating, Magruder's new heavy rail battery was protected with a breastwork of 500lb cotton bales. Magruder's plan was that the artillery should open up on the US Navy gunboats in the bay, while infantry and dismounted dragoons with scaling ladders assaulted the Union infantry occupying the wharf; all this would distract the Union sailors while two Confederate attack boats, carrying boarding parties protected by cotton bales, steamed into the bay to ram them.

John Bankhead Magruder, nicknamed "Prince John," may have been flamboyant, but his penchant for theatrics paid off for the Confederacy. After driving the Federals from Galveston, TX, Magruder made good use of the island's railroad lines; the six forts on the island, as well as that at Virginia Point on the mainland, were all joined by rail. When the Union blockading ships returned to harass the city Magruder simply loaded what guns he had onto cars and rolled them from one location to another, allowing them to fire at each stop, thereby creating the illusion that every fort contained a full battery. This ruse, along with some fake "Quaker guns," made the island appear much better defended than it actually was. (LC)

Early on the morning of New Year's Day, 1863, Magruder's guns opened the attack. The Union gunboats immediately responded with a fire heavy enough that Magruder's gun positions began to crumble. The cotton-armored rail gun, exchanging shots with the USS *Harriet Lane* at about 300 yards' range, proved no match for her. The assault infantry waded into the water with their ladders, but were soon driven back by shellfire and musketry. The Confederate attack boats were late; many of the Southern artillery crews abandoned their guns and fell back, and all seemed lost by the time the cotton-clad steamers finally came into view. However, the seaborne Confederates promptly rammed, boarded, and captured the *Harriet Lane*, then took or drove off the remainder of the Union squadron. Although Magruder's rail battery was ineffective on that occasion the Confederates were undeterred; Texas engineers constructed a second railroad gun to defend their city, this time with a turret, indicating that it must have housed a light field gun.

On the other flank of the Confederacy, BrigGen Joseph Finegan made a heavy rail battery part of his arsenal while defending Florida from Union attack. Like Magruder's gun in Galveston, Finegan's was a 32-pdr naval gun in a siege carriage mounted on a flatcar, the whole thing protected by cotton bales and pushed into action by a locomotive. After establishing a successful garrison on Amelia Island off the northeast coast of Florida, the Federals occupied and then abandoned Jacksonville several times during the course of the war, and when they held it in the spring of 1863 they built their own defensive works around the city. Finegan ordered his railroad battery to steam along the Florida, Atlantic & Gulf Central line to within 1½ miles of Jacksonville; the gun crew opened fire on the Federal defenses, but soon had to retire when Union gunboats let loose a barrage. The next day Federal columns marched out of the city to attack Finegan's troops, and once again he sent out his cotton-clad battery, this time with cavalry and infantry on its flanks. The Northerners had an armed car of their own, apparently pushed by hand and mounting a 12-pdr Parrot as well as a small

C

RAIL BATTERIES

1: CONFEDERATE HOWITZER CAR

A howitzer car was the simplest and easiest type of railroad battery to put into action, and it could be hitched to the back or, as here, to the front of a train, thanks to the coupling bar mounted at the top of the cowcatcher. This Confederate crew are manning a 12-pdr mountain howitzer on a five-stake flatcar of the Western & Atlantic Railroad, guarded by infantry who can deploy to skirmish at need.

2: UNION IRONCLAD

Some ironclad cars were only partially armored. The Union ironclad seen here, hitched at the end of a train behind a USMRR boxcar, is based on a sketch in an 1862 edition of *Harper's Weekly*. The basis is a flatcar, roughly 32ft long; the gun position has a low, inwards-slanting "prow" and sidewalls made of lengths of railroad track – "T-rails" (though actually the section was more like an I-beam) – bolted to a wooden superstructure, leaving the top and rear open. When under fire, the riflemen on board could crouch down for protection and act as sharpshooters. The artillery crew would be exposed when manning their gun; however, the great advantage to this design is that the gun, mounted on a pivot, would have a clear field of fire over a wide arc, unlike an enclosed ironclad with only three portholes to shoot from.

3: CONFEDERATE HEAVY BATTERY WITH COTTON-BALE "ARMOR"

Fortified positions protected with 500lb cotton bales were not uncommon during the Civil War; the large bale would absorb bullets and offered some protection against field artillery fragments. However, when subjected to direct US naval gunfire some of the cotton bales protecting Confederate ships were simply whisked from the deck, along with anything else in the way. Cotton could also catch fire, and defenders had to be prepared to put out the flames. This speculative reconstruction shows a 32-pdr gun mounted on a barbette carriage and placed on a heavy timber seven-axle flatbed. General John B. Magruder employed a cotton-armored heavy battery at Galveston on January 1, 1863, though it proved no match for the guns of the USS *Harriet Lane*.

1
2
U.S.M.R.R.
Nº 165
3

Before the war Joseph Finegan, a lawyer and planter, had helped construct the Florida Railroad. As a Confederate brigadier general he would try unsuccessfully to mediate between David Yulee, president of the company, and Florida Governor John Milton, who wanted to seize the company's rails for more urgent use elsewhere. Finegan was also a believer in heavy rail batteries, employing them both at Jacksonville in 1863 and at Olustee the following February. (LC)

swivel gun. The Parrot crew were busy trying to blow up a railroad culvert to prevent Finegan's heavy gun from advancing on them when a section of Florida field artillery moved up to outflank them; when the cotton-clad also came within range the Federals, heavily outgunned and caught in a crossfire, promptly retired. Thus ended one of the rare episodes when two armed railroad cars actually fought each other. The next day the Federals came out again and tried to destroy the tracks, and once more Finegan's rail battery drove them off.

At the battle of Olustee on February 20, 1864, Finegan used another heavy railroad gun. This battery – commanded by Lt Drury Rambo, and mounting a 30-pdr Parrot with a crew of 14 – was ordered to fall back some distance along the tracks of the Florida, Atlantic & Gulf Central Railroad and await orders. Rambo could not fire at the Federals from that position with any safety since there were too many Southern infantry in the thick pine forest, who would also sustain injuries from trees shattered by his heavy gun. Eventually the Northerners fell back in earnest, and Rambo was ordered to fire into their scattered regiments; the results achieved are unknown, but the only damage to Rambo's railroad battery was five cracked spokes on one wheel of the gun carriage, which apparently broke during recoil.

Probably the most famous railborne heavy piece was the *Dictator*, a 13in seacoast mortar employed by Federal forces in the bombardment of Petersburg. It was rolled down the line on this four-axle car, then moved onto a fixed platform for firing. With a 20lb propellant charge it could lob a 220lb explosive bomb nearly a mile. (LC)

A blurred but rare image of the *Dictator* in position. Just visible at far right is a pole car carrying three powder kegs; ahead of it the mortar's taller four-axle transport car butts up against the mortar platform. Left of the end of the foot plank, two men stand in the doorway of a munitions bunker cut into the hill; this bunker can still be seen today. (LC)

While such mobile heavy artillery certainly set a precedent in land warfare, its great weaknesses were its cumbersome weight and limited field of fire. Before Lee commissioned the Navy to construct his Land *Merrimac* he sent his chief engineer to inspect the roadbed along the York River Railroad to see if the tracks could withstand the weight. Even with a locomotive a heavy battery car was difficult to move, and its field of fire was limited to the same direction the tracks were laid. Despite these drawbacks, however, a 32-pdr rail battery could still move into position and open fire faster than a typical horse-drawn field battery, and with a single shot from its longer range it could deliver 64lb of explosive ordnance directly into an enemy position – a considerable threat.

Not the least of the benefits of such a weapon at that time was its psychological impact. Rail batteries provided a real boost to the morale of troops accompanying them; soldiers would write home to their wives and families extolling the merits of these heavy guns, which could advance with them and strike fear into the enemy.

LIGHT BATTERIES

Far more common were light railroad batteries or armed trains. These were usually little more than a flatcar pushed ahead of the locomotive, and fitted with any of a variety of rifled or unrifled weapons including howitzers, mountain howitzers, the standard 12-pdr fieldpiece and lighter ordnance. The light rail battery carrying one or two pieces had several advantages over

Rappahannock Bridge and Rappahannock Station being put to the torch; note the railroad water tanks at right. Burning was obviously an effective means of bridge destruction, but only if there were no enemy troops nearby to extinguish the flames; it took some time for a fire to take hold firmly enough to ensure the destruction of the trestle. (LC)

the heavy batteries: with a more forgiving recoil, lighter guns could be redirected and operated from a variety of angles, giving them a much greater field of fire. As the cars were also lighter they did not require more solidly ballasted roadbeds and extra-sturdy bridges; they put less strain on engines, thus potentially increasing speed and saving fuel. To a large extent the light rail batteries served in a defensive capacity, protecting the train itself, or guarding a crucial bridge or junction or a construction crew working nearby.

As early as May 1861, McClellan sent his forces to secure the threatened sections of the Baltimore & Ohio Railroad, which resulted in the engagement at Philippi, (West) Virginia. As a part of this operation McClellan loaded a regiment of infantry onto cars and ordered their general to mount a gun on a flatcar at the head of the train. In addition to armed

D UNION IRONCLAD AND RIFLE CAR; CUMBERLAND, MD, JULY 1864

Unlike the Sherman tanks rolling off the Detroit assembly lines in World War II, Union ironclad cars and trains were not mass produced with systematic efficiency. They were built by different designers at different locations, and certainly varied in construction; however, the armor consisting of railroad "T-rails" stacked one on top of another and fixed to a wooden casemate was probably the best and most common design. (A few of the naval vessels of the day were also armored with T-rails drilled and fastened to the wooden structure.) At the outbreak of hostilities the Union government armored a railroad battery with sheet iron and ran it on the Philadelphia, Wilmington, & Baltimore Railroad to protect work crews. The car was later given to Gen Haupt; he had little use for it, referring to it as an "elephant," although he considered bulletproof locomotive cabs indispensable.

This artist's impression shows an ironclad battery leading the Baltimore & Ohio Railroad train despatched during the Cumberland engagement; this consisted of, from front to back, an ironclad, a rifle car, the locomotive and tender, a second rifle car, and a second ironclad. According to one account, the individual pieces of T-rail comprising the armor were continuous and bent into U-shapes, which would have provided a stronger, more rounded surface at the front corners than squared sectional walls. Rifle cars were boxcars with planking cut to provide long slots for the soldiers to shoot from; heavy timber railroad crossties were stacked against the walls on the inside, making the cars rifle-proof. The locomotive and tender, the most vulnerable element of the train, were placed in the center. According to the B & O roster, their engine number 74, a Winans 0-8-0 camelback **(inset),** was destroyed in 1864, making it quite likely the locomotive in question. At nearly 30 tons, this would have been a good choice to run an armored train except for one feature – the top cab design would have placed the engine crew at greater risk from enemy fire, although it was surely armored against bullets at least.

U.S.M.R.R.
No 1693
No 711
B.&O.
74

flatcars, commanders in the field also deployed more sophisticated ironclad cars housing one or two light guns. They usually featured at least three portholes – one on each side and one in the front – so that the gun, mounted on a swivel, could fire in any of three directions. With the exception of the Confederate turret-gun car at Galveston, armored light batteries were apparently a Northern luxury.

Ironclad cars and trains were scattered across both Eastern and Western theaters of war. After Burnside's rolling stock finally arrived at New Berne, NC, in summer 1862 he brought in engineers to construct ironclad cars, which were fitted for two guns each plus loopholes for rifles. These ironclads were manned by the Marine Artillery and accompanied every train leaving the city. During MajGen Earl Van Dorn's famous attack on Ulysses S. Grant's supply depot at Holly Springs, MS, which began on December 20, 1862, his cavalrymen encountered a Union ironclad rail battery which opened up on them with a 9-pdr rifled gun. Mississippi cavalrymen tried to outflank and capture the ironclad and its locomotive but were unsuccessful, although in all the Confederates did destroy at least two locomotives and 60 cars in this operation.

Among the massive damage to the Union rail system inflicted by Confederates during the Gettysburg campaign was the destruction of at least one ironclad car, and by July 1863 the Baltimore & Ohio shops had turned out nearly a dozen ironclad batteries for Federal use. Just days after the battle of Gettysburg a lieutenant at Harper's Ferry reported that he had five ironclads, four of them with mountain howitzers and the fifth with a 6-pdr; another five were due for delivery the following day, which the lieutenant hoped would safeguard his bridge-building crews against the swarms of Southern troops falling back into Virginia.

Ironclads were designed to fight off or frighten off guerrillas and light cavalry units lacking artillery; while their armor was built to withstand a direct hit from a 12-pdr, they were never intended to engage an infantry or cavalry unit large enough to have its own artillery support. The iron car itself may have enjoyed a degree of safety, but the locomotive was always seriously vulnerable. The North experimented with various ways of armoring their engines, but found no satisfactory answer. At Haupt's suggestion, they used 3/8in sheet iron to protect the cab and some of the moving parts, but these only stopped bullets; in his book *Military Bridges*, published during the war, he noted that a single round through the boiler jacket and into the flues would render an engine effectively useless.

A well-documented engagement near Cumberland, MD, provides a near-perfect example of the limitations of the ironclad railroad battery and train. After participating in Jubal Early's Washington Raid in July 1864, BrigGen Bradley T. Johnson's cavalry brigade fought its way back to Virginia. When they reached the Potomac River they found themselves heavily engaged with Federal forces, including a B & O ironclad train commanded by Capt Peter Petrie of the 2nd Maryland Regiment (US), which had spent most of the war protecting the railroad around Cumberland. The train consisted of a locomotive and tender in the center, coupled between a pair of rifle cars, with ironclad battery cars at both ends. Bradley Johnson ordered two guns from his Baltimore Light Artillery (CS) across a makeshift bridge, even though the teams had to drag two dead horses in their harnesses before they got into position. The artillery crews unlimbered their pieces and the gunner, Cpl George McElwee, sighted in his 6-pdr on the locomotive of Petrie's train.

His first shot punched through the boiler with a terrific explosion; with the train now crippled, he managed to fire another shell straight through the porthole of one of the ironclad cars, causing a second explosion. After the Baltimore gunners sent a couple more rounds into the rifle cars Petrie and his men abandoned their doomed train, and a nearby blockhouse and infantry also surrendered. Johnson paroled the Federal prisoners, and before continuing his withdrawal he burned what was left of the train.

WRECKING THE RAILROADS

Although both sides took advantage of the train's vulnerable dependence on rails, the damage inflicted on roadways and rolling stock was not always easy to accomplish, and nor could it deny their use permanently.

The simplest method of slowing a train was placing heavy obstructions on the track. Removing a small section of rail also caused delays, but once spotted these gaps were not difficult to repair. Both sides learned to tear up long sections of track, pile up the wooden ties, place the rails across the top, then set the ties on fire to soften and bend the iron. This was temporarily effective, but the rails could often be reheated, straightened out, and spiked back into place. Not far from Corinth, MS, BrigGen S. B. Maxey suspected that Federal cavalry troopers were attempting to destroy a section of track. He sent an engine to investigate, but it did not return. When Maxey's troops arrived they found the engine driven off the tracks but unharmed. They extinguished the fire on the railroad bridge, pulled the rails off a second fire, and had everything back in order in less than a day.

In late June 1864, Federal troops under BrigGen James H. Wilson attacked three different railroad lines around Petersburg, destroying rolling stock, tracks and infrastructure. Although they ripped up fully 60 miles of track, Confederate construction crews quickly replaced it. (LC)

Members of the USMRR Construction Corps demonstrating how to twist rails using hooks and levers. Notice that the men working under the supervisor in civilian dress are black laborers, not white soldiers detailed for the job, so this photograph was taken after BrigGen Haupt had established his permanent workforce. During the war, Northerners typically referred to all black people, free or slave, as "contrabands." Note also the passenger cars in the background. (LC)

Heated rails were also bent around trees, resulting in the famous "Sherman hairpins," but this method took hours; the iron required a great deal of heat before it became pliable, and anyway it could still be restraightened. The most effective way to damage a rail in the field was not by bending but by twisting it, after which it would have to be taken back to a mill for re-rolling. The ever-ingenious Herman Haupt carried out experiments at his base of operations in Alexandria, VA; one of his subordinates discovered a quick and simple technique for turning a T-rail into a corkscrew within minutes, using a pair of horseshoe-shaped hooks, a wooden lever, a rope, and six able-bodied men.

Wooden bridges presented obvious targets, but they were still difficult to smash; Ambrose Burnside complained that after he had spent $3,000 on destroying one bridge it was still not thoroughly wrecked. (In the early 1860s high explosives were experimental and extremely dangerous; Alfred Nobel did not patent his dynamite until 1867, so Civil War soldiers relied on black powder.) Simple burning also worked, so long as the fire had time to weaken the structure sufficiently. Artillery fire sometimes proved effective; in 1863 a Confederate gun placed at right angles to an iron bridge near Cumberland, MD, brought the massive beams crashing down after 11 shots. During the Atlanta campaign a Confederate brigadier noted in his report that he would have destroyed a bridge with his artillery but he could not justify the expenditure of ammunition. Bridge destruction often fell to the cavalry, and the lack thereof left many bridges intact; a Confederate officer in Mississippi complained that he could not destroy the bridges in his sector as ordered: "Reason, no cavalry."

Brigadier General Haupt developed a cheap and portable system whereby

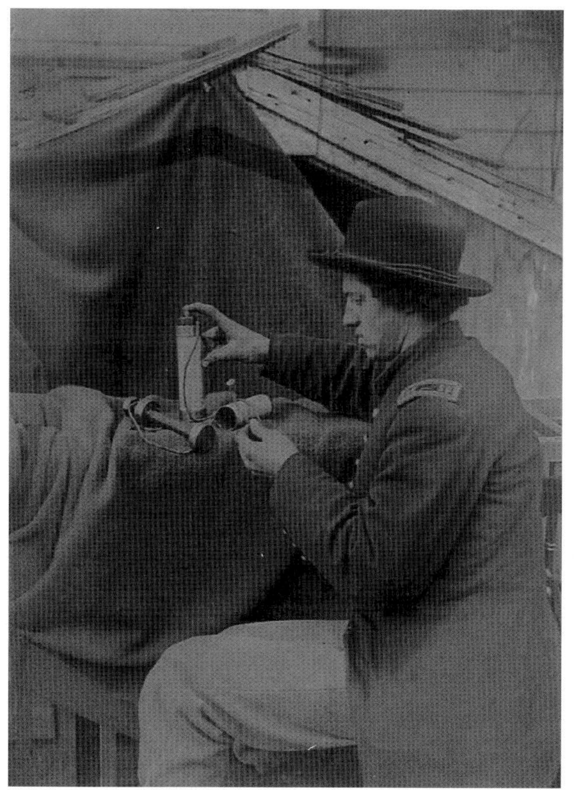

A Federal captain assembling one of Haupt's "bridge torpedoes"; and a crew demonstrating how to drill into a bridge structure and then tap the pipe-charge into the hole. Two torpedoes, one in each main brace of a panel, would bring down a Howe truss bridge, but an arch bridge needed four. Haupt suggested that two men bore holes at the same time to speed the process. (LC)

one man carrying everything he needed in his pockets could bring down a bridge in minutes. He designed a special "torpedo" (the period term for any enclosed charge) made from an 8in-long iron cylinder filled with powder and capped at both ends. Using an auger, the demolition man would drill a hole in a main support beam at one side and at one end of the bridge, insert the pipe-bomb, and light its 2ft fuse before getting to safety. Without the support beam the bridge's own weight would pull the remaining structure down.

Any locomotives and cars facing capture had to be destroyed if time and circumstances permitted, and while wooden cars burned readily enough sabotaging locomotives permanently was another matter. The cab and delicate moving parts destroyed by fire could be replaced, and, Haupt noted, to truly take out an engine one had to wreck the boiler. Early American locomotives had featured softer copper or brass boiler tubes, but by 1860 iron tubes were preferred, and these were quite fire-resistant. In 1861, after "Stonewall" Jackson burned 42 B & O locomotives and tenders and over 300 cars at Martinsburg, his lieutenants selected eight of the engines to be repaired for service on Southern lines. (Lacking a connecting line up and down the Shenandoah Valley, Jackson's men had to drag the burnt locomotives, along with six other engines, overland by horse teams.) During the fighting at Corinth, MS, an assistant superintendent of the Memphis & Charleston Railroad evacuated seven trains loaded with various government stores out of the city. When he discovered that all the bridges had been burned and his trains were trapped he ordered his engineers to run their engines off the track and dismantle them as far as possible, while the conductors burned the cars and cargoes. The engine crews smashed cylinder heads, pumps, links, valve stems, and eccentrics, removed the rods and buried all the parts in the swamp.

This man is re-straightening bent rails with a jackscrew. There was no universal specification, and "T-rail" track varied in weight from about 35lb to 68lb per yard. (LC)

The simplest way to derail an enemy train was simply to throw a switch (for British readers, "the points"), since guarding all of these was impossible. The unsuspecting crew would not know what had happened until it was too late; one conductor hauling Federal troops near Nashville claimed to have lost three engines that way. Loosening or removing just one small section of rail caused derailments, and saboteurs placed powder kegs or torpedoes under the tracks hoping to blow up a train. One Federal train leaving Saint Louis nearly experienced both of those scenarios. A powder keg exploded under the tender but did not cause any damage to the train or track; 40 cavalry troopers sent to scout ahead discovered rails missing at two different points. In November 1863 three shells were placed on a Baltimore & Ohio rail at the precise angle where the wheel of a passing train would detonate them. Two failed to explode, but the third tore up the headlight of an express train, blew out the glass in the passenger cars, dented the driving wheels, and smashed the foot board; one shell fragment was later found jutting from the boiler casing. One of the best methods of destroying an enemy train without drawing unwanted suspicion was to saw or burn through just enough of a bridge structure to ensure a collapse under the weight of a heavy load. Several trains met their fate on weakened bridges, killing both soldiers and railroad employees.

REPAIRING THE RAILROADS

Neither the North nor the South could spare the manpower to guard the thousands of contested rail miles against marauders bent on destruction.

The weight limits of portable bridge trusses were tested under the supervision of their inventor, BrigGen Herman Haupt, head of the US Construction Corps, before they were deployed in the field. (LC)

Their only viable option was to rebuild bridges and repair rails as quickly as possible, and as the war progressed the construction crews of both sides became experts at fast and efficient repairs.

When Haupt first organized his Construction Corps his laborers were soldiers detailed from other units; many were unused to construction work of any kind, some were simply unwilling to work, and they were only detailed on a daily basis. It might take Haupt all day to get a gang of soldiers organized, only for a completely different bunch to arrive for duty the following morning. When he did manage to hold onto a group of soldiers for long enough to get a whole job done Haupt pulled off some impressive feats. His temporary crew built the 150ft Ackakeek bridge in 15 hours, and in nine days they completed the Potomac Creek bridge, a trestle work 400ft long and 80ft high. While laying new rails near Fredericksburg, Haupt declared that it was a "hard-looking track" since his untrained soldiers had cut the ties anything from 4in to 1ft in thickness, but it worked. As they neared Fredericksburg in May 1862 they found several torpedoes intentionally placed on the rails, so Haupt sent ahead an engine pushing a flatcar heavily loaded with scrap iron to detonate any remaining charges.

Haupt had mixed experiences with non-specialist labor. During the first battle of Fredericksburg on December 13, 1862, Burnside sent him 200 soldiers to help construct a bridge across the Rappahannock. When the fighting started all the soldiers ran away, but the civilian carpenters and their foremen stayed at their posts and worked on for several hours, only giving up when their pulleys, ropes, and timbers were cut to pieces by Confederate shells. Haupt wanted his own men; he preferred civilians; and in the summer of 1862

A crew from Haupt's US Construction Corps are seen here putting up a truss bridge over Bull Run in April 1863, after the previous bridge had become yet another casualty of war. (LC)

he was grudgingly given his permanent Construction Corps. From the thousands of black refugees in Washington DC, Haupt selected the most willing and able he could find and organized them into squads of ten men each, with supervisors and foremen drawn from Army officers, NCOs and white civilians. His gangs became so adept that they built five bridges ranging from 60ft to 120ft in length in just one day. During the Gettysburg campaign they repaired all 19 bridges on the Northern Central in a matter of days, and while the battle was raging they were busy reconstructing the branch line between Gettysburg and Washington; less than a day after the battle ended Haupt had reopened communications with Washington.

Initially Haupt sent his crews into the forest to cut timber for the bridges, and had them haul the wood to the building site using 200 oxen with ox-

E

REPAIR TRAIN

In this imagined scenario, Union forces advancing into territory from which Confederate troops have retreated are faced with a cut telegraph line and a demolished bridge. The construction train – with a howitzer car pushed ahead of the locomotive – carries a load of Gen Haupt's prefabricated 60ft timber bridge trusses **(inset 1)**; although the standard flatcar was around 32ft long, some were constructed to 65ft length to accommodate such loads. The first vehicle down the line is a handcar with a telegraph repair crew – a civilian specialist, accompanied by a couple of engineer soldiers, carrying tools and a spool of new wire to restring the cable. Large handcars **(inset 2)** required four men to propel them by working the handles geared to the axles; since they were sent ahead to scout the line they often needed to be able to retreat at speed, and under the right conditions a handcar could outrun a horse. The construction train waits for the village at the river crossing to be reconnoitered for Confederate rearguards or a forgotten outpost, by infantry skirmishers disembarked from the train **(inset 3)** and by an accompanying troop of screening cavalry. If they run into serious opposition, the train can retreat back down the tracks.

A fortified railroad bridge over the Cumberland River near occupied Nashville, TN. A bridge with its own protected guardhouses and gate would deter local resistance or a small body of cavalry, but not troops with artillery support, or a "ram" – a runaway locomotive and burning cars. (LC)

chains and wheels. He later built a stockpile of 60ft trusses that could be loaded onto flatcars and, if necessary, pulled by the oxen and their drovers, jokingly referred to as "Haupt's horned cavalry." He also designed military truss bridges with interchangeable prefabricated parts that did not require pre-fitting in the shops. Using portable rail-straighteners in the field, Haupt's crews could repair several miles of bent (although not twisted) rail in a single day; those that were bent too far were set aside to save time until they could be taken back to a workshop or field facility where they could be reheated and hammered back into shape.

On the Confederate side, simply detailing soldiers to construction duty also brought mixed results. Lacking a separate construction corps, the

Confederate Railroad Bureau relied on the Engineer Bureau to repair bridges and tracks. From the beginning of hostilities the South relied on black crews to rebuild bridges and roadbeds since they were, to a large extent, the men who had been doing the construction work before the war. The number of black men – free or slave, hired or impressed – working with the South's army engineers dwarfed the numbers working for Haupt, and Gen Lee gave priority to repairing rail lines. The Engineer Bureau suffered from the same labor shortage as the rest of the Confederacy, and as late as February, 1865 – less than two months before Appomattox – the head of the bureau, J. F. Gilmer, told the government that he needed 29,000 more black men, not counting teamsters and cooks. (He might as well have asked for 29 million.)

What the military engineers and their black crews lacked in manpower they made up for in skill and efficiency. Carpenters and laborers shaped timber for prefabricated portable bridge spans in a large yard in Richmond, and similar preparations were made in other centers including Atlanta and Macon, GA. Official Confederate correspondence makes several references to "duplicate bridges;" this may have been simply another term for the prefabricated spans, but the reports certainly imply that the bridges and trestlework would be repaired and then an exactly sized duplicate would be made and kept in readiness for the next time that bridge was destroyed. During the Atlanta campaign LtGen John Bell Hood ordered his chief engineer to have bridge timbers ready for rebuilding all the spans between Atlanta and Tennessee, and also to build duplicate bridges for all the existing ones in the army's rear that were most likely to be put to the torch.

Not long before Sherman's destructive advance to Atlanta he paid a similar visit to northern Mississippi. Although Confederate trains steamed

Here Union troops are setting up a communications line during the battle of Fredericksburg. A signal telegraph machine inside the two-wheeled wagon is wired into the telegraph line, while two men run off additional wire from the heavy spool. (LC)

Men of the USMRR's construction and transportation crews are repairing a broken axle on the tracks of the Loudon & Hampshire Railroad in March 1863. This is a good view of the rear of a boxcar, with the brakeman's ladder, handwheel and perch. As a precursor to the caboose, which had not officially come into existence yet, trains often pulled a modified boxcar known as the "conductor's car," which served as an office or even a rolling repair shop. The workers seen here, both white and black men, wear civilian clothing. (LC)

out of Meridian, MS, with millions of dollars' worth of government supplies and a good deal of their rolling stock, Sherman's forces still found plenty of immobile property to wreck. After he pulled back, the Confederate engineers and their crews came in and repaired all the damage along a 100-mile stretch of railroad in just over 25 days. After the fall of Atlanta, Sherman split his army, sending part of it to the sea and the other part back toward Hood's position, where they could rip up the railroads in northern Mississippi yet again; this time Confederate crews repaired 4 miles' worth of bridges and 10 miles of track in six days.

RUNNING THE RAILROADS

Even in peacetime, keeping trains in operation during the steam era required a significant number of employees with a diversity of skills, and the war imposed greater demands. About half the employees of railroad companies in the antebellum South were black men, and during the war the number rose dramatically as more and more white men found themselves, voluntarily or otherwise, in Confederate uniforms. While Southern conscription laws were more generous in granting exemptions for railroad employees than were those in the North, the loss of skilled men still proved a heavier burden for Southern carriers. Northern companies had a healthy reserve of unemployed manpower to draw upon for replacements, but the South did not – at the outbreak of war the population of the North was nearly 2½ times that of the South.

This is obviously no place to discuss the wider topics of slavery and racial relations, but a few facts about the black contribution to Southern railroading must be stated, since they often contradict stereotypes. Black railroad men were important to both sides, but extremely important in the South. Southern companies typically owned a few slaves outright, but secured the bulk of their slave labor force by hiring men from a slave owner through a broker, as was common practice for many types of businesses throughout the South. Slaves in the urban centers where many railroad companies were based sometimes lived and worked with much more autonomy than their counterparts toiling as field hands. They could sometimes choose the employment they wanted, make contracts so that they could earn their own money, and set up their own homes. Railroad companies also hired a large number of free black men. (In 1860 there were nearly 132,000 free black people living in the 11 states that would comprise the Confederacy; some of them, such as the owners of coastal boats, were quite successful businessmen, and held slaves themselves.) While most black railroad employees worked as freight handlers and roadway laborers, significant numbers – both free and slave – were highly skilled boilermakers, blacksmiths, carpenters, machinists and mechanics, and the Southern railroad companies were glad to have their services. They also worked in large numbers aboard trains as brakemen and firemen.

WATER AND WOOD

A locomotive could not run without water, but in many cases the train crews could not depend on the availability of watering stations equipped with large wooden tanks; everything that could keep a train running was targeted for destruction by the enemy, including watering and fueling stations. Some historians have painted a rather condescending picture of Confederate train crews who had to refill their tenders using buckets of water pulled from nearby streams, but Southern carriers certainly maintained their own watering stations in peacetime. For instance, a slave named Harkless, along with another fellow, manned the station on the Virginia Central some 4 miles from Gordonsville; Harkless pumped the water, and he also cooked meals for the crews who stopped to refill their tanks. Sometimes Northerners also had to rely on buckets and creeks. During the Gettysburg campaign Haupt knew that the watering and fueling facilities would be wrecked by the Confederates, so in order to keep the trains moving he sent ahead 400 railroad workers with lanterns, buckets and a train loaded with cordwood to refuel the other engines. During the fall of 1862, Haupt had himself ridden aboard a train equipped with just two buckets. The Manassas Gap line had been abandoned for some time and the grass had grown so tall around the rails that the drivers were losing traction. The engine soon ran out of sand, and some of the soldiers were sent ahead to place pebbles on the rails to be crushed for traction. Before long they had exhausted their water as well, and it had to be carried from streams and puddles. Considering that the tender held anywhere between 1,000 and 2,000 gallons, refilling with just two buckets must have been a distinctly tedious task.

Another problem was contaminants in the water, and Haupt complained that the guards posted to protect water and fuel stations sometimes caused as much damage as Confederate raiders. For some reason the unruly Union guards broke switch stands, ripped up sidings, and burned the cordwood meant for the locomotives. They also took baths and washed their clothes in the streams that fed directly into the water tanks; when heated, the soapy water foamed up in the boilers and temporarily disabled the engines.

For the South, fuel presented a greater problem than water. Before the war railroad companies typically bought cordwood from private contractors, but when the war put many of these men in uniform the companies had to cut and transport their own wood supply. The South had plenty of trees but not enough laborers to cut them, despite the conscription of black men. In addition to its numerical superiority in manpower, the North, which ran trains on both wood and coal, enjoyed another great advantage over the South – effective control of America's waterways. It was no coincidence that Northern military staging areas were located near navigable waterways both along the Atlantic seaboard and the Gulf coast, as well as along the inland river systems. Any coal or cordwood that could not be transported by train could be shipped by boat to supply points such as Vicksburg, City Point, and New Berne.

In addition to the laborers required to load and unload freight, railroad companies on both sides needed large numbers of men to work in the maintenance shops. Keeping their engines and cars in pristine condition was impossible for Southern carriers during the war, and the rolling stock on Northern lines also showed a marked deterioration. While the Northern companies certainly made money hauling troops and war supplies as well as normal commercial freight, the heavy demands of wartime traffic coupled with the loss of skilled employees resulted in a higher degree of wear and tear. The annual reports of the B & O, for example, show that the company was continuously repairing engines and cars or building new cars. The situation in the South was even bleaker. Between the trade embargo and the blockade, the South, which had relied heavily on Northern and British manufacturers, lost their main suppliers of parts and lubricants (even locomotive headlamps were not spared – they ran on New England sperm whale oil.) At one point 50 Confederate locomotives were put out of service simply from a lack of tires. By necessity, many Southern carriers became as self-sufficient as possible. One company in Virginia, which had relied on whale-oil lubricants and Cincinnati bacon, built its own smokehouse and bought its own pigs; the cured pork fed the employees, and the rendered oil lubricated the machinery. Carriers in Alabama produced lubricants derived from grain alcohol. Nevertheless, despite the deficiencies in manpower, fuel and parts, not to mention the ravages of war, the superintendent of a Georgia carrier declared that his company had moved more tonnage in the last three years of the war than in any previous three-year period.

A Union telegraph operator using a signal telegraph machine in Fredericksburg, VA. It was in 1861 that the first message was flashed right across the continent from coast to coast, and the telegraph quickly became a serious military tool. The Lincoln administration circumvented the sometimes dubious reports coming up the usual military channels from its generals, and set up a telegraph service completely separate from the US Army Signal Corps. This US Military Telegraph Service fed a direct line into the War Department in Washington DC, allowing Lincoln to get a second opinion as to what was really happening at the front. Surprisingly, the Confederate Congress – which would not allow President Davis to take full control of the railroads until it was far too late - did allow him to take control of the telegraphs as early as May 1861, and he put Postmaster General John H. Regan in charge. The aim was to prevent the leaking of information about military operations, since the telegraphs were used by the military, the newspapers, and to some extent by private citizens. (LC)

THE TELEGRAPH

Working closely with the world's fastest land transportation was the world's fastest communications system. The electrically powered telegraph could deliver a message as fast as the sending operator could tap out the "dots and dashes" and the receiving operator could transcribe the Morse code into English. Thousands of miles of wire telegraph lines spread across the country, usually next to the railroad tracks. The North, again, owned the vast majority of the telegraph lines and employed most of the workforce; many of the lines operating in the South were owned by Northern companies, and split along the new borders on the outbreak of the war. The American Telegraph company, one of the primary operators in the Atlantic coastal states, became the Southern Telegraph Company within the Confederate borders.

In peacetime the telegraph was one of the railroads' most important safety devices, allowing the various stations to report rapidly any dangers along the roadway and to keep accurate track of inbound trains, which was crucial – especially on the many single-track lines. During the war the telegraph lines were frequently cut, and several serious accidents resulted from a combination of downed telegraph lines and military commanders who ordered the trains to move despite the protests of civilian railroad employees. Herman Haupt considered the telegraph a luxury when it happened to work; when the lines were down he refused to wait for repair crews to get them back up, sending runners ahead with signal flags to keep his supply trains moving safely.

As well as breaks in the line another problem was eavesdroppers, since both sides frequently engaged in wiretapping. One man armed with a "pocket telegraph," which was nothing more than a waterproof case containing a Morse key and sounder, could literally hook into the uninsulated line, listen to the traffic and even transmit his own deceptive messages. Telegraph operators were so adept at their job that they could actually recognize one another's signals simply from their "fist" – their individual mode of keying – and some wartime wiretappers even taught themselves how to imitate a particular operator's style. Perhaps the best-

A Union telegraph lineman at work; the job of repairing fallen or cut lines was often dangerous, since if it was attempted within sight of the enemy it attracted sharpshooters. Although the figures are not precise, it is estimated that the telegraph employees working in the field suffered about the same casualty rate as front-line combat soldiers. (LC)

A Union blockhouse with camp quarters beside it, guarding the Nashville & Chattanooga Railroad near occupied Chattanooga. This was built to defend the line against MajGen Joseph Wheeler's cavalry. (LC)

known wiretapper and Morse impersonator was John Hunt Morgan's telegraph operator George Ellsworth, aka "Captain Lightning," whom the Confederate raider kept close at hand wherever he went. Although both sides often used ciphers or codes, a great deal of disinformation (and even jokes) still flowed down the lines. On one occasion J. E. B. Stuart telegraphed the Union Quartermaster General to tell him that the Federal mules he had captured were poor-quality animals and were not well suited to move the Federal wagons that he had also captured.

Repairing the telegraph lines was often a hazardous task, since a lone man clinging near the top of a telegraph pole presented a tempting target. Repair crews were often despatched by train or handcar and were accompanied by a trained operator who could immediately report the situation to commanders

A substantial two-storey blockhouse beside the Tennessee River. Such buildings contained sleeping quarters, storerooms, and cooking facilities, and were built sturdily enough that the small garrison could hold out for some time against anything except assault by regular troops with strong artillery support. (LC)

as soon as the line was back up. Cutting the wires in a combat zone could be as dangerous as repairing them, and Heros von Borcke (the swashbuckling soldier-adventurer from Prussia who ended up riding with J. E. B. Stuart's cavalry) left a vivid anecdote. Late in the Peninsular campaign Stuart ordered von Borcke to cut a telegraph wire, but when the Prussian reached the designated spot he found an entire company of Federals drawn up in line of battle. Von Borcke called in a squadron of cavalry and attacked the Federals, who fell back, but were by no means routed. While both sides exchanged fire, a teenaged Confederate volunteered for the risky duty; he climbed onto von Borcke's shoulders, shimmied up the pole, and slashed the wire with his saber while Federal bullets smacked into the wood around him.

When there were no enemy troops present Haupt recommended that the wire should be cut at frequent intervals but not left dangling. He suggested that a saboteur should climb the pole, cut the wire and then reconnect the ends uselessly with insulated wire, hiding the false connection under the insulators to make it more difficult for the Southerners to find the break.

FORTIFICATIONS

Both sides attempted to guard key bridges, tunnels, stations or sections of the tracks with earthworks, "cotton forts," blockhouses, infantry or cavalry units or sometimes just a single emplaced gun. As the war progressed, blockhouses of various designs sprang up next to railroad structures across both Eastern and Western theaters. Some were fairly simple one-storey affairs not much more sophisticated than a "bombproof," but many were given a second floor to allow the defenders to fire from an elevated position. US Army engineers built nearly 50 blockhouses near the various bridges and depots of the Baltimore & Ohio, and some locations had more than one – the Rowlesburg Bridge was protected by no fewer than four. These sturdy, dug-in wooden structures could withstand the impact of bullets and even, to some extent, field-gun shells.

Blockhouses and battery positions had the disadvantage, especially in the South, of tying down numerous troops needed more urgently elsewhere. During fluid campaigns field commanders would often place artillery pieces near a bridge or depot, or send a small detachment of infantry or cavalry to ward off roaming enemy cavalry. While blockhouses, batteries, and temporary or permanent guard detachments were effective against small numbers of attackers they were obviously no match for major units on

An interior view of a Confederate fort guarding the Western & Atlantic Railroad in Atlanta, GA. The earth ramparts are revetted with planking and consolidated with sandbags, and there is an external *chevaux-de-frise* of X-shaped pointed stakes set along poles. (LC)

A train rolling over some serious trestlework near the fighting at Petersburg. The two boxcars are loaded with troops, both inside and riding the roofs, and the flatcars behind may be carrying artillery. A "bombproof" shelter, used as an ammunition store and occasionally as an officers' position, lies between the two trees in the center. (LC)

the move. While campaigning in northern Virginia in August 1862, "Stonewall" Jackson's forces drove off the Union guards left at Bristoe Station on the Orange & Alexandria Railroad. Jackson captured two trains approaching the station unwarned; he then turned his forces on Manassas Junction, capturing nine artillery pieces, 300 prisoners, nearly 200 horses, 50,000 pounds of bacon, and thousands of barrels of salt pork, flour, and corned beef.

TRAINS IN BATTLE

AMBUSH

While the railroad batteries were intentionally sent into combat, the majority of battle-damaged rolling stock were ordinary engines and cars that wandered into the wrong place at the wrong time. The crews and passengers aboard non-combat vehicles inadvertently steaming into harm's way were routinely fired upon. Although trains hit by small-arms bullets, and even by shells from field batteries and the occasional gunboat, usually survived the ordeal, the same cannot be said for many of the people aboard. While Jackson held Bristoe Station during the Second Manassas campaign a USMRR engine, the *Secretary*, limped back into Federal hands after being attacked and riddled with bullets by 500 Confederate cavalrymen. A few weeks later, at Haupt's request, the Federals began their experiments with locomotive armor.

During the Peninsular campaign Heros von Borcke and the advance guard of the 19th Virginia Cavalry descended on a Federal station on the

York River Railroad and were about to wreck the place when they noticed a train coming. They placed obstructions on the track and scattered along both sides of the embankment in order to attack it when it stopped. The train, loaded with Union soldiers mostly in open cars, slowed but had not quite stopped when the first shots rang out. As the Virginia troopers began to fire in earnest the engineer opened the throttle; some of the Union soldiers jumped off, while the others fired back or crouched as low as they could. A captain rode up and shot the engineer with a blunderbuss; von Borcke emptied his revolver at the fleeing Federals while chasing the train, but the horses could not keep pace with it; it crashed through the barricade and got away with all of its cars.

This 0-8-0 camelback was one of many B & O locomotives and cars burned by "Stonewall" Jackson's forces at Martinsburg in 1861. The cab is burned away but most of the locomotive remains largely intact – which is why Jackson was able to put eight of these machines back into service for Confederate use further south. (Courtesy B & O Railroad Museum)

As MajGen Philip Sheridan tore through the Shenandoah Valley in March 1865, a Virginia Central crew were ordered to take their engine, the *Albemarle,* into the Valley to deliver a barrel of whiskey to Waynesboro station, but by the time they reached it the Confederate cavalry were already in full retreat. On their return trip east they stopped at Greenwood Station to pick up some cars loaded with government supplies, but as they pulled through Greenwood Tunnel and into the clearing with the seven cars – three ahead of the engine and four behind – they spotted a sea of Federal cavalry. The conductor, fireman, and brakeman all jumped; the engineer was about to do the same when he decided to take his chances and try to save the train. He jerked on the throttle, but it was stuck and he couldn't pick up speed, so he lay flat on the footboard as the cavalry attacked. Since the train was traveling no faster than the horses, one trooper was able to ride alongside the *Albemarle* and empty his seven-shot carbine into the engine and tender; one bullet ripped through the seat cushion while another

1
U.S.M.RR
2
3

one punctured the tank. (It was a high shot - if it had been lower in the tank the water would have leaked out, and once the water level drops too low a hot boiler will explode.) Before the trooper could reload the engineer jumped up, managed to unstick the throttle, and sped away with a derisive pull on his whistle.

Lieutenant General Richard Taylor, who had assumed command of the remnants of the Army of Tennessee in January 1865, was busy funneling his railroad equipment out of central Alabama and into Mississippi as 10,000 Federal troopers descended on his position. Nathan Bedford Forrest rode up to him, with blood literally dripping from his clothes and horse, and told Taylor to leave immediately or be captured. As Forrest wheeled his mount and galloped off Taylor climbed aboard a small yard engine, which had an all-black crew. Federal cavalry rode into range before they could get full steam up and fired off an erratic fusillade without effect, but the little locomotive picked up speed and rushed the army commander to safety.

One of the most devastating attacks on a train did not involve cavalry. While mounted troops could briefly chase a train, a large body of infantry in line of battle along with their artillery support could deliver significantly more firepower. In October 1862 the Federals launched a combined Army/Navy attack designed to smash the Charleston & Savannah Railroad near Coosawhatchie, South Carolina. Three hundred men of the 48th New York Infantry, along with 50 from the 3rd Rhode Island Artillery and 50 Army engineers, hoped to destroy the Coosawhatchie Bridge, the telegraph network, and anything else they could find. They were about to begin the destruction when they heard a train whistle, and skirmishers soon discovered that it was a troop train loaded with Confederate soldiers. The commander of the expedition, Col William Barton, ordered his men into position to attack. The bulk of the Confederates on the train were from the 11th South Carolina Infantry, most of them packed onto flatcars where

F CONFEDERATE "RAM" ON THE BALTIMORE & OHIO RAILROAD

This imagined scenario shows an attempt to block a tunnel on a stretch of Union-held track. Not only were bridges and stations fortified and guarded, but key tunnels needed protection as well. (In 1864, while trying to slow Gen Sherman's march through Georgia, Gen Joseph Johnston hoped to destroy an important railroad tunnel; hearing this, one Confederate joked sourly that it was pointless, since Sherman doubtless carried duplicate tunnels.)

In a desperate situation when a track was blocked at both ends and a locomotive could not be saved, the engines were sometimes turned into 20-ton missiles. An unmanned locomotive with the throttle jammed open would continue to pick up speed until it derailed, possibly destroying enemy property and personnel. Adding burning cars to the mix would increase the destruction, especially if they were loaded with ammunition like the ones at Savage's Station. Burning cars were also left on wooden bridges in order to eliminate the rolling stock and the bridge itself.

(Inset 1) Captured locomotive with cotton-bale armor for the cab and steam dome, and "pitched roof house car" packed with inflammables and perhaps explosives and set ablaze as a rolling incendiary bomb.

(Inset 2) Timber blockhouse of the type designed to guard choke points on the B & O Railroad. Measuring about 30ft on a side and standing some 32ft tall to the roof peak, it is basically two box-shapes set one on top of the other at a 45-degree angle. The jutting corners of the second floor included trapdoors in the floor so that the men upstairs could shoot down at anyone getting too close to the building. Rifle slits on both floors were 12in deep on the inside but tapered down to 3in on the outside, for ease of aiming and protection. A trench was dug out around the entire building and the spoil piled high around the walls for added protection; a surrounding abatis or *chevaux-de-frise*, and angled earthworks at the entrance, prevented a direct rush at the door. This substantial little fortress is built and provisioned for long-term occupation, with a brick chimney stack and wooden ventilator trunks in the roof.

(Inset 3) Surprised Union artillerymen in a two-gun sandbag battery protecting the track attempt to bring a 12-pdr Napoleon to bear on the runaway locomotive.

This small yard engine was badly burned during the fall of Richmond. The wooden section of the cab has been completely consumed, leaving only the iron uprights and bolts, but the boiler itself may be salvageable. (LC)

they were completely exposed. When they came within range the Northerners ripped into them with musketry, canister and grape shot; some 25 or 30 men either fell or jumped from the train, which was not about to slow down long enough for them to climb back aboard. The fireman was killed outright and the engineer was either killed or disabled, so a third Charleston & Savannah employee, probably the conductor, had to step in and take the controls. The casualty returns for the Coosawhatchie engagement list the 11th SC as having 4 killed, 15 wounded, and 2 missing. Amidst the shooting, a black man – probably a brakeman – leapt from the train and dashed back to prevent a second train from meeting the same fate.

DELIBERATE ENGAGEMENT

Trains were not always the unsuspecting victims of attack, and were often used in a tactically offensive capacity. A Union colonel operating in Missouri in 1861 learned that Confederates were tearing up the track two miles from his position; he put a company of infantry on a train and immediately ordered it to the scene, where the mobile infantry quickly drove off the Confederates. In the meantime, more Southerners were wrecking the rails in the opposite direction; the colonel tried the same tactic with a second train, but the second group of Confederates was protected by artillery. When this opened fire the train commander ordered a retreat, on the premise that an engine and cars were more valuable than a small section of track, and the colonel agreed. During the same operation the colonel also demonstrated another important railroad tactic – the use of cavalry screens. While transporting his infantry on the cars he ordered the engineers to drive slowly so that the cavalry could keep pace and protect them.

Cavalry and sometimes infantry flankers might have slowed the trains down, but they were very useful in hostile territory. In September 1864 the Federals moved a string of trains from Bolivar Heights to Winchester, VA, using the 12th Pennsylvania Cavalry as a screening force. In December of the same year a Confederate train in northern Alabama ran into a Federal cavalry unit; the train was forced to retreat, but before long it came back with its own cavalry support, and a small battle ensued.

While operating his trains near Manassas, BrigGen Haupt frequently put guards aboard, who would dismount when they reached an uncertain area and fan out as skirmishers. He felt that if his guards ran into a larger force they could always fall back to the train, which could quickly take them and itself out of harm's way. Often a train with its own skirmishers would be sent to run well ahead of other trains hauling troops, supplies, or even construction crews; just prior to Second Manassas, Haupt sent a pilot engine with guards riding on two flatcars to make sure it was safe to move troops. Following the battle of Chancellorsville, Haupt's trains on the Orange & Alexandria were attacked so frequently that a pilot engine with sharpshooters proved useless, and he had to put 30 to 50 guards on every single train on the line in order to fight off the partisans.

RECONNAISSANCE

Throughout the war trains and engines quite often served as reconnaissance vehicles. During the Second Manassas campaign Haupt lost contact with all the troop trains he sent to Catlett's Station, so he sent a lone engine to cautiously investigate. He could not send any more troops or supplies until the empty trains returned, and after several nerve-racking hours he finally

This locomotive hulk has been thoroughly stripped; it sits on two sets of emergency wheel-trucks (bogies), and is missing the cowcatcher, headlamp, smokestack, sandbox, part of the steam dome, the rods, cylinders, the leading truck, and all of its wheels. The fact that the cab remains would indicate that it was not burned, although some cabs were made of metal. This engine may have been stripped for parts, or simply to prevent the enemy from using it. (LC)

learned that the troops at Catlett refused to get off the trains in spite of their orders. Four days later Haupt sent out a telegraph- and rail-repair crew under the protection of 200 sharpshooters; the crew was ordered to rebuild the bridge over Pohick Creek, and use the telegraph to give continuous reports on the Confederate strength and positions at Manassas. During the Coosawhatchie engagement Federal raiders had cut the telegraph wires, and before BrigGen William Walker could commit his troops he needed to know what he was up against, so he sent two couriers along with a reconnaissance locomotive.

BALLOONS

Perhaps the most interesting reconnaissance system involved an engine, flatcars, and a balloon. Tethered observation balloons were used quite extensively during certain campaigns, some employing hot air but most of them filled with gas. Early in the war the latter had to be inflated with coal gas or illuminating gas at a city's gasworks facility and then transported to the observation site. (The Northerners eventually developed a portable field generator that produced hydrogen gas, allowing them to inflate their balloons anywhere on the ground or on the deck of a ship.) Edward Porter Alexander, the brigadier general perhaps best remembered for his artillery bombardment on the third day of Gettysburg, was also one of the Confederacy's most

G

MISCELLANEOUS EMPLOYMENT

1: CONFEDERATE GEN ALEXANDER'S OBSERVATION BALLOON; SEVEN DAYS' BATTLES, JUNE 1862

The Richmond & York River Railroad flatcars carrying BrigGen Edward P. Alexander's balloon and its operating equipment were most likely pushed ahead of the engine, with the balloon itself as far away from the smokestack as possible, since a spark or cinder would have proven disastrous for the delicate varnished silk envelope filled with 7,500 cu/ft of flammable gas. (The multicolored appearance of the balloon was due to the fact that it was made from a patchwork of silks intended for dressmaking. A rumor was begun that it was in fact made from dresses donated by patriotic Southern ladies, but although the myth endures today, it is sadly untrue.) Wood-burning locomotives were notorious for spreading dangerous sparks, causing hundreds of thousands of dollars' worth of property damage annually – not only to company cars, bridges, and stations, as well as the commercial freight carried, but also to barns, fences, and trees along the tracks. During the 19th century inventors took out more than 1,000 patents for new designs of spark arrestors and smokestacks, but none of them ever solved the problem. To maintain a working fire the steam system required a draft, and any arrestor efficient enough to catch all the sparks would inevitably inhibit the free flow of oxygen. Almost every Civil War-era illustration of a passenger train or a hospital train depicts a freight car, usually a boxcar, coupled directly behind the tender to offer passengers some shelter from the soot and cinders.

Alexander's tethered flights usually reached about 1,000ft altitude, and crew members worked the windlass (seen covered on the second car) to bring him back down; this car also carries the small basket, ballast bags, and coils of rope. Crews often had to work fast to keep their observer and balloon as safe as possible. Just above the tree line, when ascending or descending, wartime balloonists had to pass through the danger zone – the airspace within range of enemy shells. Artillerists turned anti-aircraft gunners loved to shoot at balloons, especially when they had nothing else to do. Union soldiers would take bets with each other, gambling on the odds that their own balloons would get blasted out of the sky.

2: CONFEDERATE NAVY & MARINE CORPS BOARDING PARTY; NORTH CAROLINA, FEBRUARY 1864

In late January 1864, Confederate sailors and marines armed with cutlasses and pistols launched a daring raid on a Federal gunboat at New Berne in conjunction with George Pickett's overland assault. Traveling nearly two days by rail from Petersburg, VA to Kinston, NC, the group finally put their cutters into the Neuse River, where they rowed to New Berne and then captured and destroyed the USS *Underwriter*. (They wore white cotton armbands to identify each other at night.) On both trips, coming and going, they tied their boats upright to the flatcars and rode in them as if they were gliding over waves instead of rails. They presented quite a spectacle as they passed from town to town, and like good sailors and marines they hopped out of their boats at every opportunity to flirt with the local ladies. Here we imagine them on the return journey, carrying their wounded with them.

1
R. Y. R. R.
No 81
R. & Y. R. R.
No 76
2
W. & W. R. R.
No 22
W. & W. R. R.

prominent balloonists. During the Seven Days' Battles, Alexander made numerous ascents both day and night. The balloon, inflated at the Richmond Gas Works, had to be transported to the observation site; Alexander felt that he could not move it through the woods or along the narrow roads stretching out from the city for fear of tree branches puncturing the delicate silk envelope – a proven hazard. Alexander reasoned that the best way to transport an inflated balloon was to secure it to a railroad car and send it along the open roadway by locomotive. (Eventually the Federal units moved too far away for observations from the rail line to be useful. After Alexander had finished making observations from the gunboat *Teaser* on the James River, the vessel and the deflated balloon were captured by the Federal gunboat *Maratanza* on the morning of July 4, 1862.)

The scourge of the Union railroad and telegraph employees working in disputed territory: the Confederate guerrilla. Fast-moving and hard-hitting, guerrillas or "partisan rangers" could strike at a poorly defended work crew, then blend back into the local population. (LC)

COMMAND CARS

Generals frequently commandeered cars or whole trains for their command staff and sometimes for their own personal transportation. It was important for generals to rendezvous with their fellow commanders as quickly as possible, and they often arrived well ahead of the bulk of their forces. When Longstreet rode to Georgia to support Bragg during the Chickamauga campaign he arrived with part of his staff around 2pm on September 19; two hours later their horses arrived on a different train. After the close of his Shenandoah Valley campaign "Stonewall" Jackson needed to get from Gordonsville to Richmond to discuss his next move with Lee but, as usual, he didn't want anyone to know what he was up to. Confiding his plan to only one other officer, his chief of staff Maj Robert Dabney, Jackson secured a yard engine and a postal car. Leaving their horses behind, the two boarded the car and Jackson crawled into the mail clerk's bunk and promptly fell asleep. Generals may have enjoyed their own cars but this privilege certainly did not enjoy universal approval, especially in the democratically minded South. In June 1862, Gen Beauregard and his staff occupied two cars as they rolled into Mobile, AL; Kate Cumming, a hospital matron who was crammed into one of the other cars, was absolutely incensed that perfectly healthy men should spend a leisurely ride in the ladies' car and a baggage car while the sick and wounded were crowded miserably into the rest of the train.

Several workmen riding down the tracks on a lightweight handcar. At center, note the men grasping the protruding levers (visible as pale uprights) that work the gearing connected to the axles. The man in the dark coat is probably grasping a brake handle. (Courtesy B & O Railroad Museum)

Generals not only requisitioned existing railroad cars, they also had headquarters cars specially built. The USMRR shops in occupied Nashville turned out an armored car for MajGen George Thomas; this bulletproof vehicle was 50ft long and included an office, kitchen, dining compartment, sleeping quarters, and even a toilet.

HANDCARS

Handcars and pole cars were employed extensively across the railroads of antebellum America, and were pressed into military use in great numbers. Both types were human-powered; the handcar featured a gearing mechanism that had to be pumped or cranked, while the simpler pole car was literally "punted" along the tracks with a long pole. The little double-axle cars could cost anywhere from one-sixth to one-twelfth as much as a standard freight car, and owing to their lightness and method of propulsion they were in many ways more versatile. Used as maintenance vehicles before and during the war, they were frequently sent out to investigate and repair downed telegraph wires – a dangerous mission in a contested area. One Confederate crew in Louisiana barely escaped with their telegraph equipment and handcar when a Federal raiding party came upon them while demolishing the Vicksburg, Shreveport, & Texas Railroad.

Apart from burning, another way of deliberately sabotaging a locomotive that could not be saved from the enemy was to send it crashing off a bridge. This Federal ordnance train at Savage's Station in late June 1862 was set on fire and plunged into the Chickahominy River over what was left of Bottom's Bridge. Note the six-wheel tender – rather unusual for this period. (LC)]

Burnside used shipped-in handcars to haul supplies during his North Carolina operation, and they were also carried aboard trains, being used to carry messengers when the telegraph lines were inoperable or sent in emergencies to warn incoming trains of danger. During and after battles any available handcars were used for medical evacuation. On August 27, 1862, during the Second Manassas campaign, BrigGen George W. Taylor's New Jersey Brigade was cut to pieces. Taylor himself suffered a serious leg wound, and his men rolled him by handcar to Burke's Station; thence he went by train to Mansion House Hospital in Alexandria, where surgeons carried out an amputation, but he died on September 1.

Senior officers and important civilian officials used handcars for personal transport. The president of the Richmond & Danville Railroad, Lewis Harvey, sustained a variety of injuries when he and the black employees working his handcar crashed into the back of a stationary passenger car. On September 12, 1862, a freight train on the Wilmington & Weldon plowed into the handcar carrying William S. Ashe, the former head of the Confederate Railroad Bureau; mangled beyond recognition, he died two days later. Both of these accidents happened at night, and the freight train that mortally injured Ashe did not have a working headlamp.

HOSPITAL TRAINS

Medical evacuation trains were interchangeably known as hospital trains, ambulance trains, or sick trains. They had two basic functions: those more properly called ambulance trains, which transported the sick and wounded to hospitals, and those that transported the hospitals themselves.

As the war intensified a system of mobile hospitals became a necessity, especially for Confederate forces. Prior to the war the only significant military facilities were the marine hospitals scattered up and down the coast, but the war brought a seemingly overnight explosion of hospital accommodations. Both government and private hospitals sprang up; specialized facilities were later established to treat patients with particular diseases or disorders, and orthopedic hospitals and mental health facilities were also established to assist recovering soldiers. Civil War women are well remembered for their heroic and tireless work in the nursing field, although in fact the overwhelming majority of nurses were men. Before the war the best-trained female nurses came from the Catholic sisterhoods who maintained hospitals in the private sector; army doctors from both sides initially felt that women were unsuited for military hospital service but, undaunted, Northern and Southern women demanded their inclusion. They were soon granted official status within the army hospital systems, and assigned to specific duties. The forceful Dorothea Dix volunteered for duty as soon as the war broke out, and was quickly placed in charge of recruiting and managing all the female nurses in the Union army. The male Union nurses came from the ranks, although some were civilian volunteers.

In the South, white women served as matrons or nurse supervisors in charge of a ward; black women typically worked as laundresses, and many of the nurses were detailed from among the sizeable pool of convalescent white soldiers, despite their frequently being unequal to their tasks. Able-bodied male nurses were resented by other Confederate soldiers, who generally felt that they should be serving at the front. Their government shared this view; aside from the doctors, the only white men of military age exempt from combat duty were the hospital stewards, who primarily served as pharmacists. Otherwise, any soldier unlucky enough to wind up in a Confederate hospital was more often than not nursed back to health by black men, who would eventually make up more than half of the Confederate nursing staff.

Federal soldiers load their wounded onto flatcars at Fair Oak Station after the battle of Seven Pines, June 1862. The cars would be covered with straw and blankets, and a gangplank made the transfer easier. The patients suffered an excruciating ride in the two-wheeled "avalanche" ambulance, as shown in the center; these were eventually phased out and replaced with the four-wheeled ambulance, which was not much better. Branches were cut and fixed to the flatcars to provide some shade for the wounded. The locomotive pictured here is the *Exetor*. (LC)

During a battle, doctors established field hospitals just out of range of enemy artillery. In theory, the wounded were carried back to the field hospitals for immediate treatment, and from there they were sent by horse-drawn ambulance and commissary wagons to an evacuation or "wayside" hospital on a railroad line, usually close enough to the rail station that the wounded could be transferred by litter (stretcher). Trains transported the wounded to general hospitals in Richmond, Lynchburg, Washington, Baltimore, Philadelphia and many other locations North and South. Northern casualties often had to travel longer distances than their Southern counterparts and they were frequently transferred to hospital ships, although many doctors felt that their patients got a smoother ride on a train than on a ship at sea.

After major engagements both sides usually lacked enough wagons and trains to carry the numerous casualties. Ideally, wounded soldiers at recently established wayside hospitals would not spend more than a couple of hours waiting for train transportation, but they were sometimes left without food, water, or medical attention for miserably long periods. Depending upon their location, some wayside hospitals existed for the duration of the war while others were merely temporary affairs. The North established several wayside hospitals in Frederick, MD, and after the battle of Sharpsburg the Frederick staffs received and treated the wounded for months. Following the battle of Gettysburg more than 4,000 Union casualties were too badly injured to move, so the medical staff set up a facility known as Letterman Hospital, which remained for four months along the rail line east of town. It was named for the capable Jonathan Letterman, Medical Director for the Army of the Potomac, one of whose many achievements involved the control of medical transportation. At the beginning of the war the Quartermaster Corps managed this, but Letterman saw to it that the Medical Department controlled its own ambulance wagons and hospital ships.

The North built scores of hospital rail cars of various gauges. Some had seats that could be dropped down to form a bed, and others were designed to hold three tiers of litters bunk-style along both side walls. The litters were suspended by large rubber bands, and the most severely wounded men were kept on the bottom tier. The US Sanitary Commission provided a number of hospital cars equipped with 24 stretchers, a water tank, sink, wash basin, and a copper boiler to prepare coffee, tea, and soup. They also carried extra clothing for the patients, and were connected by speaking tubes so that the train's surgeon could communicate with the nurses in the various cars. Like the cars, the trains also differed. One Union hospital train operating on the Nashville & Chattanooga line included three ambulance cars, three boxcars, one mail car, and one passenger car for patients who wanted to sit up. Another train included five ambulance cars, a kitchen car, a surgeon's car, a dispensary car, a passenger car, and a conductor's car. Of course, when a battle brought a heavy flood of casualties there were not enough specialty cars to provide the transportation, and medical officers had to load their patients onto anything that could move.

Historians have generally shortchanged the South's hospital trains, but the Confederacy certainly ran them on a regular basis and from an early date. In October 1861 the Virginia Central built two ambulance cars designed to hold 44 casualties each, distributed over 22 single and 11 double berths. As early as November 13, 1861, Dr F. W. Roddy, assistant surgeon in the Provisional Army of the Confederate States, took charge of an ambulance train operating between Manassas and Richmond; Dr Roddy continued to run his train until he was captured in a Richmond hospital on April 3, 1865. He employed different nurses throughout the war, but at one point his staff included four free black men and two white men. Interestingly, free black men serving as nurses were paid $20 a month – almost twice the wages of a white infantryman, who only drew $11 a month. By comparison, white women serving as hospital matrons received $30 to $40 a month. The existing quartermaster records show that Dr Roddy rented four rooms in Richmond and requisitioned 3½ cords of fuel wood monthly, which would indicate that his nurses lived with him.

The state of Georgia drafted a resolution allowing a hospital train to run regularly on the Western & Atlantic Railroad. Assistant Surgeon Francis Dennis took charge of the train, but unlike Roddy, Dennis and his staff spent the war at various locations including rented rooms in Allatoona and Marietta, GA, and Chattanooga, Tennessee. Sometimes the supervision of sick and wounded soldiers on trains fell to the doctors stationed at the wayside hospitals. While working at a station on the Richmond & Danville line, Surgeon Wellford was ordered to take railroad officials and Confederate police and board every incoming passenger train to determine if the furloughed soldiers were fit for travel. Wellford stated that he had to board the freight trains as well since so many soldiers traveled on them. Some of the men escaped the doctor's control, no doubt preferring to recuperate or die at home.

Early in the war medical personnel from both sides frequently placed their casualties in freight cars cushioned with nothing more than straw and blankets. During the battle of Chickamauga, Dr Samuel H. Stout, the highly

In both the North and the South each hospital train usually carried a surgeon while each ambulance car carried a nurse, to keep the car clean and well supplied with water and to tend the patients. The enlisted man on the right, next to the wash basin on its fluted stand, displays the sleeve insignia of a US Army hospital steward (though apparently reversed in this image): a green half-chevron edged with yellow and bearing a yellow caduceus device. Note the rubber bands secured at varying levels on the support posts, allowing the litters to shift in transit without touching the ones directly behind or in front of them. (LC)

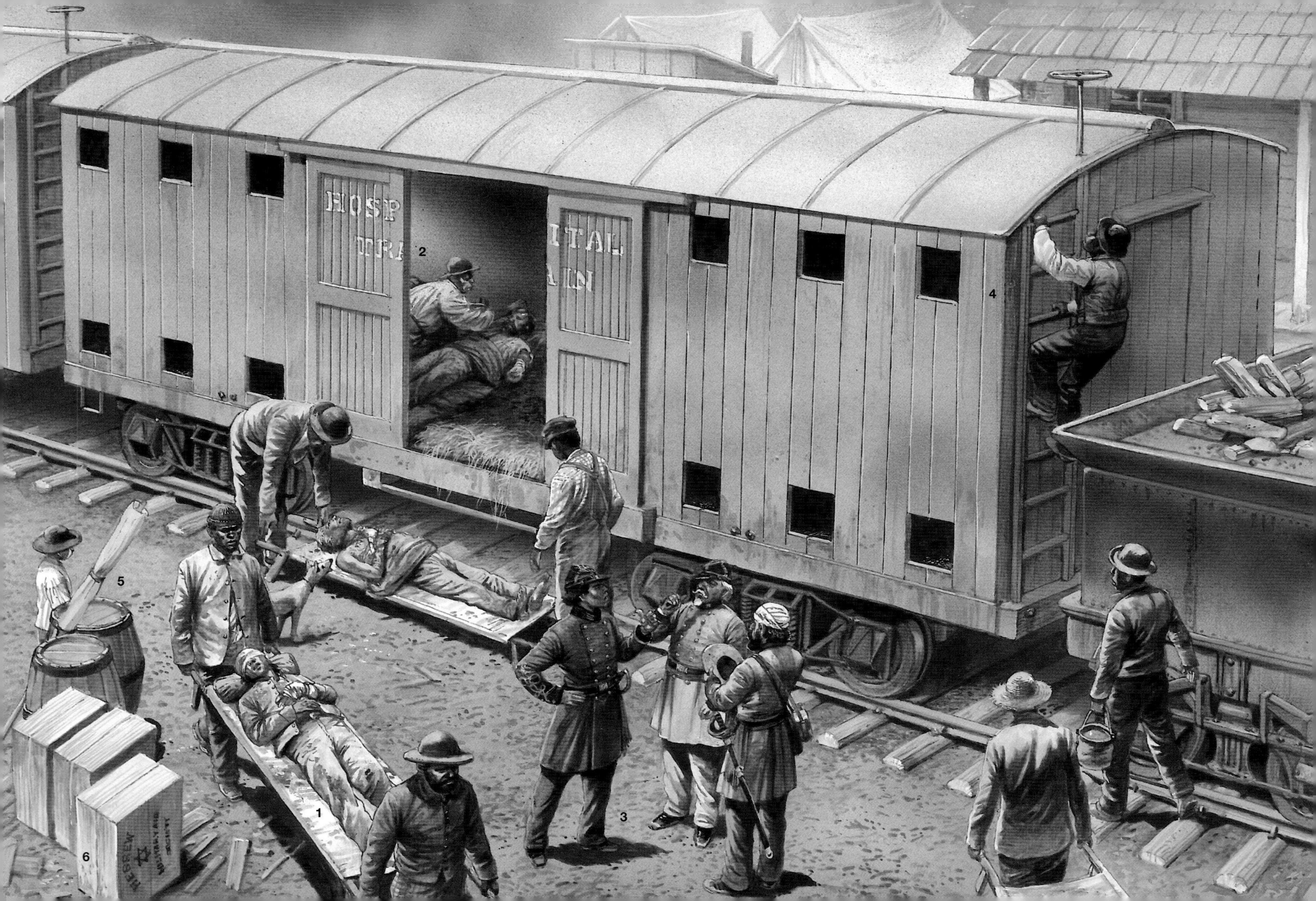

HOSP
TRA
ITAL
IN
HEBREW
1
2
3
4
5
6

proficient Chief Medical Director for the Army of Tennessee, noticed that someone under his command had placed the wounded in commissary wagons filled to the brim with pine-tops and covered with a blanket; as it turned out, this simple improvement on the straw method provided a more comfortable way of evacuating the wounded than anything offered by the latest technology in wagon springs. The wounded soldier was tucked into the nest of straw, pine-tops, prairie grass or whatever soft material the staff could

A Union hospital train – with a single boxcar hastily identified, and three passenger cars – making the run from Chattanooga to Nashville. (LC)

H

CONFEDERATE HOSPITAL TRAIN

Dr Stout's simpler yet more comfortable ambulance car, using straw rather than slung litter/bunks, featured ventilation holes cut near the roof and the floor. In this case a baggage car, coupled directly to the tender, has also been modified to evacuate wounded soldiers.

1: Black men frequently served as ambulance-drivers and litter-bearers in the Confederate army. During various battles a significant number of black men working as teamsters for the Quartermaster Department were shifted to ambulance duty, transporting the wounded to waiting trains at wayside stations.

2: In addition to caring for the patients and supplying water, the nurses on board ambulance cars changed out the bedding, cleaned the car, and kept it stocked with fresh bandages. Patients also had to be fed; but while Civil War doctors knew that a proper diet was essential to health, they had an appallingly poor understanding of the causes of disease and infection. One Confederate doctor noted after the war that it was fortunate that he eventually ran out of sponges and had to resort to rags, since the sponges were loaded with germs that spread from one patient to the next.

3: Two medical officers – an assistant surgeon ranking as captain, and a surgeon ranking as major – confer with an infantry officer. Although Confederate uniforms were extremely varied, there is plenty of evidence to show that Confederate doctors at least tried to keep themselves properly outfitted. One surgeon mentioned in a letter to his wife that while he had an officer's uniform the only material he could get was brown; his brigade later issued gray cloth for the officers, but there was not enough to go round, so they had to draw lots for it. Doctors were frequently left behind to care for the severely wounded, which meant inevitable capture; wishing to be recognizable as non-combatants, they made sure that they had their identifying green sashes.

4: In the days before automatic brakes and couplers the brakemen held the most dangerous job on the train. In peace and wartime alike they frequently fell to their deaths, and the trainmen who had to join cars with the old link-and-pin couplers often had a few fingers missing. Each wagon had its own brake, and the brakeman had to climb up to the roof of baggage cars to turn the brakewheel by hand.

5: Confederate surgeons were also expected to carry yellow hospital flags and red ambulance flags, and to display them conspicuously for easy identification.

6: Numerous charitable organizations across the North and South contributed to the war effort. Matron Kate Cumming often received food packages for her patients and staff from the Hebrew Military Aid Society based in her adopted hometown of Mobile, Alabama. The aid society packages often included spices, wines, preserves, oysters, and sardines; clothing and money were also donated to help the patients.

gather locally. Stout found that the sprung horse-drawn ambulance wagons bounced the patient around agonizingly; applying the principle to the railroad, Stout got rid of all his "so-called railway ambulance cars" with their tiered berths, and replaced them with boxcars complete with one or two feet of straw on the floor. Stout reasoned that not only did the soldiers in the top berths have to breath the rank air expelled by the sick and wounded on the lower berths, but the train's jolting knocked the top tiers around painfully and sometimes even threw men from their bunks. Placing the wounded on the floor kept them at the car's center of gravity and gave them an easier ride.

Sickness cases always far outstripped battle casualties; during Sherman's famous march through Georgia his combined armies suffered nearly 23,000 wounded and 4,423 dead from enemy action, but 43,000 men fell sick in the Army of the Cumberland alone. Of those, 25,000 had to be evacuated to the rear, and some 60 per cent of the wounded also had to be sent back to the general hospitals in occupied Chattanooga.

The Army of the Cumberland regularly ran three trains comprising 10–12 hospital cars each, apart from freight trains pressed into service as medical transports. The Medical Department set up a large mobile tent hospital, and every time the armies established new bases closer and closer to Atlanta and later Savannah the tent hospital was packed onto trains and sent forward. During the fighting around Big Shanty, however, the Federals were in such a hurry to get their wounded out that they bypassed the forward surgical hospital and simply transferred the casualties from the field hospitals directly onto the trains. By the time the hapless soldiers had made the 36-hour, 100-mile journey to Chattanooga many of their wounds were already infected with gangrene.

Facing Sherman, the Confederate Army of Tennessee maintained an even more complex network of mobile hospitals. With well over 60 hospitals distributed over hundreds of miles, Dr Stout decided that instead of abandoning a hospital he would, when necessary, pack up everything from the senior surgeons to the forks and spoons and send the entire complement by train (or occasionally by horse and wagon) to a safer location. The new sites along the

The Scottish-born Kate Cumming emigrated to Canada with her family when a child but later settled in Mobile, AL, and served as a matron in the Confederate medical service. She describes the evacuation of a mobile army hospital as a series of movements. First, the sick were properly cared for and sent off by train, then the tents were dropped. While the staff packed up and the cooks prepared rations for the journey, more trains would arrive to carry off the hospital equipment piecemeal. Within a few hours the whole hospital was gone, on its way to a safer location. (LC)

railroad line were carefully chosen, for access to clean drinking water, firewood, and at least a small local population who could sell or donate food for the patients. Some of the hospitals were set up in existing buildings while others relied on tents, new construction, or any combination of the three. Many of the mobile hospitals were named after people and not places, since they might remain at a given site for anything between a matter of months and a matter of days. In 1864 the Flewellen Hospital spent five months in Barnesville, six weeks in Opelika, nine days in Mobile, and two days in Corinth.

Kate Cumming, who worked as a matron under Stout's jurisdiction, left an excellent diary describing her experiences with the Confederate mobile army hospitals. On her journey from Cherokee Springs to Newnan, GA, she remarked that there were too many trains to count. She compared the hospital movements to a contra dance, where the head couple has to jump to the foot, and she noticed that when the hospitals were ordered to pack up and leave it usually meant that the entire army was about to evacuate that sector. Sometimes the hospitals operated fairly close to one another, and Matron Cumming mentions that the Bragg Hospital rode on the same train as her own Newsom Hospital, which at times could accommodate 500 patients. While the bunks, mattresses, furniture, tents, medicines, most of the patients, and staff were crammed into the uncomfortable cars, one very important part of the hospital had to be left behind – the severely sick and wounded. One of Kate Cumming's nurses, obviously a detailed white soldier, was terrified at the thought of having to stay behind and tend a dying patient; he had already been in a Union prison camp, and didn't want to go back. A black nurse might have stood a better chance. When Federal raiders overran one of Stout's hospitals before it could evacuate, the staff and the walking wounded got away but a black woman and a nurse, feigning illnesses of their own, stayed behind so that they could take care of the real casualties who were unable to leave.

Confederate prisoners at Chattanooga, about to take an unwanted trip in the freight cars. Just as in 20th-century wars, captured officers and enlisted men were sent to separate prison camps in order to break down the command structure and hopefully discourage escape attempts. These prisoners are fairly well clothed with pale caped overcoats, probably sky-blue US issue previously captured from Union stores. When the train rolls out, numerous guards will ride the roofs of the boxcars. (LC)

The Baltimore & Ohio RR was a victim of geography. While the company's lines, workshops, and stations lay south of the Mason-Dixon Line, Maryland, northern Virginia, and soon-to-be West Virginia were highly contested areas due to the location of the US capital. The B & O became the hardest-hit private carrier serving the North. Just days after Virginia officially seceded, "Stonewall" Jackson was ordered to secure Harper's Ferry. As Jackson and his troops sat along the B & O lines they watched loads of coal rolling from Cumberland to Washington, DC, but the Confederate government hesitated to destroy the B & O because many of the company's investors in Maryland were pro-Southern. Finally, in June 1861, the Richmond government turned Jackson loose, and the wrecking began. This picture, taken years after the war, shows an 0-8-0 camelback hauling a string of iron coal cars. (Courtesy B & O Railroad Museum)

FURTHER READING

The following is a select list of works dealing with Civil War era railroads. For a comprehensive bibliography, see David M. Stokes' article: "Railroads Blue & Gray – Rail Transport in the Civil War, 1861–1865: a Bibliography" in *National Railway Bulletin* Vol 65, No.5 (2000). Due to potential interest in black Confederates, one work on that subject is also included.

Abdill, George B., *Civil War Railroads* (Seattle, WA; Superior Publishing Co, 1961)

Black, Robert C. III, *The Railroads of the Confederacy* (Chapel Hill, NC; University of North Carolina Press, 1952)

Brewer, James H., *The Confederate Negro: Virginia's Craftsmen and Military Laborers, 1861–1865* (Tuscaloosa, AL; University of Alabama Press, 1969)

Cumming, Kate, *Kate: The Journal of a Confederate Nurse* (Baton Rouge, LA; Louisiana State University Press, 1998. R/p of 1959 volume edited by Richard Barksdale Harwell)

Haupt, Herman, *Reminiscences of General Herman Haupt* (Milwaukee, WI; Wright & Joys Co, 1901)

Johnston, Angus J. II, *Virginia Railroads in the Civil War* (Chapel Hill, NC; University of North Carolina Press, 1961)

Koenig, Alan R., *Mars Gets New Chariots: The Iron Horse in Combat, 1861–65* (Lincoln, NE; Universe, 2006)

Schroeder-Lein, Glenna R., *Confederate Hospitals on the Move: Samuel H. Stout and the Army of Tennessee* (Columbia, SC; University of South Carolina Press, 1994)

Swank, Walbrook D. (ed) *Train Running for the Confederacy: 1861–1865 – An Eyewitness Memoir* (Shippensburg, PA; Burd Street Press, 1990)

Turner, George Edgar, *Victory Rode the Rails: The Strategic Place of the Railroads in the Civil War* (Indianapolis, IN; Bobbs-Merrill Co, 1953)

Weber, Thomas, *The Northern Railroads in the Civil War: 1861–1865* (New York, NY; King's Crown Press, 1952)

White, John H. Jr., *A History of the American Locomotive – Its Development: 1830–1880* (New York, NY; Dover Publications,1979. R/p of Johns Hopkins Press 1968 edn)

At center, behind the man in the top hat, lie the burned remains of an Orange & Alexandria RR train. The better part of the locomotive has survived, but the rest has been reduced to axles and wheels. (LC)

INDEX

References to illustrations are shown in **bold**. Plates are shown with page locators in brackets.

ambulance cars **55**, **56**, **57**, **H(58)**, 59, 60
ambulance trains/wagons 54, 56–7, 60
ammunition trains, destruction of **20**
armor, types of
  "cotton-bale" 19, 21, 22, **C3(23)**, 24, **F(46)**, 47
  sheet-iron 10, **A2(11)**, 26, 28
artillery 16, 21, 22, **C1–3(23)**, 28–9, 30, 43, **44**
Atlantic & North Carolina Railroad 15

baggage cars 16, 52, **H(58)**, 59
balloons, rail transport of 50, **G1(51)**, 52
Baltimore & Ohio Railroad 6, 8, **8**, 9, **9**, 26, **D(27)**, 28–9, 31, 32, 40, 43, **45**, **F(46)**, 47, 62, **62**
barbette carriages 22, **C3(23)**
barges, carriage of rolling stock **14**
Bottom's Bridge **54**
boxcars 6, 8, **8**, **9**, **38**, 50, **G(51)**, 56
  use of 8, 9, **12**, **14**, 16, 22, **C(23)**, 26, **D(27)**, **44**, **59**, 60, **61**
brakeman's hand wheel/ladder **9**, **38**
brakemen, role of **H(58)**, 59
Burnside's Wharf **16**

casemates (rail batteries) 19, 20, 26, **D(27)**
casualties **55**, **56**, 57, **57**, **H(58)**, 59–60
Charleston & Savannah Railroad 47–8
City Point railroad yard 5, 7–8, **10**, **12**
coal cars 6, 9, 16, **62**
coal, hauling/use of 4, 6, 40, **62**
command cars 52–3
commissary wagons 56, 59–60
communications links, setting up of **37**
conductors (cars) 6, 31, 48, 56
Confederacy/South: rail system 5, 15–16
  construction of connecting lines 9
  effects of embargo/blockade 9, 16, 40
  employment of black men 38–9, **38**
  influence of state governments 8–9
  strategic importance of 8–9
  track gauges 6
  wartime speeds of locomotives 12
Confederate Navy 9, 19, 20, 21, 22, 24, 25, 50, **G(51)**
construction crews/trains 26, **29**, 33, **E(34)**, 35–7, **38**
Cumberland engagement 26, **D(27)**, 28–9
Cumming, Matron Kate 52, 59, **60**, 61

demolition men (bridges) 31, **31**
dispensary and dump cars 6, 56

engineer soldiers **E(34)**, 35

field artillery/guns **B(18)**, 19, **19**, 20, 24, 25, 28, **F(46)**, 47
  on railroad cars 17, 21, 22, **C1–3(23)**
Finegan, BrigGen Joseph (C) 22, 24, **24**
flatbeds (seven-axle) 22, **C3(23)**
flatcars **5**, 6, 22, **C1–2(23)**, 25, 26, 28, 33, **E(34)**, 35, 36, **44**, 47–8, 49, 50, **G1–2(51)**, **55**
Florida, Atlantic & Gulf Central Railroad 22, 24
fortifications (rail defense) 29, **42**, 43–4, **43**, **44**, **F(46)**, 47
Fredericksburg, battle of (1862) 33, **37**
freight cars **5**, 50, **G1(51)**, 57, 59, **61**

guardhouses **36**, 43, 49
guerrillas/"partisan rangers" **52**
gunboats 14, 21, 22, 44, 50, 52

handcars 15, **E(34)**, 35, 42–3, 53–4, **53**
Haupt, BrigGen Herman 7, 8, 26, 28, 30–1, **31**, 33, **E(34)**, 35, **35**, 36, 39, 44, 49–50
horse-teams **12**, 15, 31
hospital cars/trains 10, **A(11)**, 54–8, **H(58)**, 59–61, **59**
hospital flags **H(58)**, 59
hospital stewards, sleeve insignia **57**
hospital tents **20**
house cars as rolling bombs **F(46)**, 47
howitzer cars 17, 22, **C1(23)**, 25, **E(34)**, 35

Illinois Central Railroad 14
ironclad cars/trains 4, **B(18)**, 19, 22, **C2(23)**, 26, **D(27)**, 28–9

Jackson, Gen Thomas "Stonewall" 13, 31, 44, **45**, 52, 62

Lee, Gen Robert E. 8, 9, 12, 15, 17, **B(18)**, 19–21, **20**, 25, 37, 52
locomotive engines 47
  armor protection 10, **A2(11)**, 19, 26, 28, **44**, **F(46)**, 47
  attacks on 6, 10, 19, 21, 28–9, 31, 32, 33, **44**, **45**, **45**, **F(46)**, 47, **54**, **63**
  boiler jackets 10, **10**, **A1–3(11)**, 28, 29
  cabs 10, **A2(11)**, 19, 28
  capture and use of 6, 7, 10, 31, **45**
  colour schemes/decoration of 10, **A1–3(11)**
  cowcatchers 22, **C1(23)**
  crews, risks faced by 4, 5, 26, 44, 45, 47, 48
  fuel/water consumption 6, 39–40
  and railroad batteries **B(18)**, 19, 20, 21, 22, **C1–3(23)**, 26, **D(27)**
  smokestacks 10, **A1–3(11)**, 50, **G1(51)**
  steam domes **10**, **F(46)**, 47
  stripping of for parts **49**
  types of 9, 31
  4-4-0 6, **10**
  4-4-0 "General McCallum" 10, **A1(11)**
  0-8-0 camelback **45**, **62**
  Exetor **55**
  Hayes 4-6-0 "camelback" 4
  Secretary 44
  "Talisman" 10, **A2(11)**
  The General 6
  Winans 0-8-0 camelback 26, **D(27)**
  USMRR service 7, **10**, 14, **14**, 15
Loudon & Hampshire Railroad **38**
lubricants, Southern production of 40

Magruder, MajGen John B. 20, 21, **21**, 22
mail/postal cars 16, 52, 56
maintenance vehicles, use of 53, **53**
Manassas Gap Railroad line 12, 13, 39
McClellan, MajGen George B. 14, 17, 19, 20, 26, 28
medical evacuation trains 5, 54–8, 59–61
medical officers **H(58)**, 59
Memphis & Charleston Railroad 17, 31
mobile hospitals 54–5, 60–1
mortars, rail carriage of 17, 24, **24**, **25**
munitions bunkers **25**

Nashville & Chattanooga Railroad **42**, 56
New York & Erie Railroad 7
New York Railroad 25

Ohio & Mississippi Railroad 14
Orange & Alexandria Railroad 12, 44, 49, **63**
ordnance trains, destruction of **54**

passenger cars 6, 16, **30**, 56, **59**
Peninsula Campaign 14, 17, 19, 20–1, **20**, 44–5
Petersburg 4, 5, 8, 12, 15, **17**, **19**, 24, 29
Philadelphia & Reading Railroad 10
Philadelphia, Wilmington & Baltimore Railroad 26
"platform" cars 5, 16

pole cars 6, **10**, **13**, **25**, 53

railcars **B(18)**, 19, **F(46)**, 47
railroad batteries (heavy) 17, **17**, **B(18)**, 19–21, **19**, **20**, 22, **C1–3(23)**, 24–5, **24**, **25**
railroad batteries (light) 25–6, **D(27)**, 28–9, **E(34)**, 35
railroad bridges 26, 29
  construction/repair of 7, 33, **E(34)**, 35–7, **35**
  destruction of 7, 21, **26**, 30–1, **31**, 33, **E(34)**, 35, 36, 38, 47
  explosive charges 30, 31, **31**, 32
  fortification of **36**, 43
Railroad Bureau 8, 9, 15–16, 37
railroad cars 17, **B(18)**, 19–20, **19**, 21, 22, **C1–3(23)**, 24–5, **24**, **25**
railroad system
  1861 extent of 5
  financing of/currency notes 5, **6**
  government requisition of lines 7
  as military transportation system 7
  ownership of 6, 7
  safety standards on 6
  strategic importance of 8–9
  track gauge variations 6
  tactical capacity/versatility of 4–5
railroad tracks 6, 8, 9, 13
  components/laying of 6, **10**, 22, **C2(23)**, 26, **D(27)**, 29, 30, **30**, 32, 33
  repair of 29, **29**, 30, **30**, **32**, 36–7
  sabotage/wrecking of 7, 24, 29–32, **29**, **31**
Railways and Telegraph Act 7, 8
repair trains **E(34)**, 35
Richmond & Danville Railroad 54
Richmond & York River Railroad 14, 19, 50, **G1(51)**
Richmond, Fredericksburg & Potomac Railroad 16
rifle cars 26, **D(27)**, 28

sandbag batteries **F(46)**, 47
Savage's Station **B(18)**, 19, 20–1, **20**, 54
screening cavalry, Union use of **E(34)**, 35
Seven Pines, battle of (1862) **55**
Sherman, Gen William T. 6, 16–17, 37–8, 47, 60
siege guns, transport of 21, 22, **C1–3(23)**, 24
signal telegraph machine **40**
skirmishers 21, 22, **C1(23)**, **E(34)**, 35, 49
surgeons (cars) 56, 58, **H(58)**, 59–60
swivel guns 17, 22, **C2(23)**, 24, 28

telegraph lines/service 7, 40
  cutting of **E(34)**, 35, 41, 43, 50
  military use of **40**, 41–3
  repairing of **E(34)**, 35, 41, **41**, 42–3, 52, 53
tenders 6, 10, **10**, **A1–3(11)**, 26, **D(27)**, 28, **31**, 39, **54**
transport ships **12**
troop carriers/transport cars 4, 12–13, **13**, 14, 15, 16, 17, **24**, **25**, 26, **44**, 45, 47–8
tunnel-blocking **F(46)**, 47

US Construction Corps, role of **30**, 33, **E(34)**, 35–6, **35**
US Military Railroads 5, 7–8, 10, **10**, **12**, 14, **14**, 22, **C2(23)**, **38**, **44**, 53

Vicksburg, Shreveport & Texas Railroad 53
Virginia Central line 13, 39, 45, 47, 56

watering stations/tanks **10**, **26**, 39
"wayside" hospitals 56, 57, **H(58)**, 59
Western & Atlantic Railroad 6, **6**, 9, 22, **C1(23)**, **43**, 57

yard engines 47, **48**, 52
York River Railroad 20, 45